Chicken Soup
for the Girlfriend's Soul

CHICKEN SOUP FOR THE GIRLFRIEND'S SOUL

Celebrating the Friends Who Cheer Us Up, Cheer Us On and Make Our Lives Complete

Jack Canfield
Mark Victor Hansen
Chrissy and Mark Donnelly
Stefanie Adrian

Health Communications, Inc.
Deerfield Beach, Florida

www.hcibooks.com
www.chickensoup.com

We would like to acknowledge the many publishers and individuals who granted us permission to reprint the cited material. (Note: The stories that are in the public domain or that were written by Jack Canfield, Mark Victor Hansen, Mark Donnelly, Chrissy Donnelly or Stefanie Adrian are not included in this listing.)

Toasting Rye Bread. Reprinted by permission of Commonwealth Foundation. ©1996 Commonwealth Foundation.

Nancy and Caroline, Saying Good-Bye and *The Other Woman.* Reprinted by permission of Sally Friedman. ©2003 Sally Friedman.

I Found My Best Friend After Forty Years by Marjorie Conder. From *Good Housekeeping,* Issue: 1/95 (pg 68).

The Friends Who Saved Me. Reprinted by permission of Jill Goldstein. ©2003 Jill Goldstein.

Bosom Buddies. Reprinted by permission of Alice Collins. ©2004 Alice Collins.

(Continued on page 287)

Library of Congress Cataloging-in-Publication Data is available at the Library of Congress.

©2004 Jack Canfield, Mark Victor Hansen, Chrissy and Mark Donnelly, and Stefanie Adrian
ISBN 0-7573-0154-1 (trade paper)

Publisher: Health Communications, Inc.
3201 S.W. 15th Street
Deerfield Beach, FL 33442-8190

Cover design by Andrea Perrine Brower
Inside formatting by Dawn Von Strolley Grove

In loving remembrance we dedicate this book to Gina Michelle Kosmas, a loving daughter, sister, wife, mother and dear friend.
May her essence live on in her children.

We also dedicate this book to all of our other girlfriends who have touched our lives.

Contents

3. BEING THERE FOR EACH OTHER

4. SPECIAL MOMENTS

5. UNEXPECTED FRIENDS

Acknowledgments

The path to *Chicken Soup for the Girlfriend's Soul* has been made all the more beautiful by the many "companions" who have been with us along the way. Our heartfelt gratitude to:

Our families, who have been chicken soup for our souls!

Inga, Travis, Riley, Christopher, Oran and Kyle Canfield for all their love and support.

Patty, Elizabeth and Melanie Hansen, for once again sharing and lovingly supporting us in creating yet another book.

Our publisher, Peter Vegso, for his vision and commitment to bringing *Chicken Soup for the Soul* to the world.

Patty Aubery and Russ Kamalski for being there on every step of the journey, with love, laughter and endless creativity.

Lisa Drucker for editing the final readers' manuscript and being there for help along the way.

Kelly Garman and Dena Jacobson for their care and loving determination to secure our permissions and get everything just right.

Barbara LoMonaco and Gretchen Stadnik for nourishing us with truly wonderful stories and cartoons.

D'ette Corona for being there to answer any questions along the way.

Patty Hansen, for her thorough and competent handling of the legal and licensing aspects of the *Chicken Soup for the Soul* books. You are magnificent at the challenge!

Laurie Hartman for being a precious guardian of the Chicken Soup brand.

Veronica Romero, Teresa Esparza, Robin Yerian, Jesse Ianniello, Jody Emme, Debbie Lefever, Michelle Adams, Dee Dee Romanello, Shanna Vieyra, Lisa Williams, Gina Romanello, Brittany Shaw, Dena Jacobson, Tanya Jones, Mary McKay and David Coleman, who support Jack's and Mark's businesses with skill and love.

Bret Witter, Allison Janse, Elisabeth Rinaldi and Kathy Grant, the editorial department at Health Communications, Inc., for their devotion to excellence.

Terry Burke, Tom Sand, Lori Golden, Kelly Johnson Maragni, Randee Feldman, Patricia McConnell, Kim Weiss, and Paola Fernandez-Rana, the marketing, sales, administration and PR departments at Health Communications, Inc., for doing such an incredible job supporting our books.

Tom Sand, Claude Choquette and Luc Jutras, who manage year after year to get our books translated into thirty-six languages around the world.

The art department at Health Communications, Inc., for their talent, creativity and unrelenting patience in producing book covers and inside designs that capture the essence of Chicken Soup: Larissa Hise Henoch, Lawna Patterson Oldfield, Andrea Perrine Brower, Anthony Clausi and Dawn Von Strolley Grove.

Debbie Merkle, Jane St.-Martin and Dianne Zimmerman at Donnelly Marketing Group, for encouragement and support along the way.

All the *Chicken Soup for the Soul* coauthors, who make it

such a joy to be part of this Chicken Soup family.

Our glorious panel of readers who helped us make the final selections and made invaluable suggestions on how to improve the book: Jennifer Brown, Tricia Callaway, Anne Carter, Denise Cavanagh, Jane Coffin, Craig Coleman, Kristan Fazio, Nancy Gibbs, Karen Henderson, Jill Holland, Nicole Holliday, Donna Johnson, Mike Johnson, Suzy Kay, Vicki Landingham, Kathy Marie, Lori May, Bob Neale, Jeanne Neale, Vickie Rayson, Diane Smith, Holly Stiggleman, David Wilkins, Deb Zika, Lindsey Buechler.

And, most of all, everyone who submitted their heartfelt stories, poems, quotes and cartoons for possible inclusion in this book. While we were not able to use everything you sent in, we know that each word came from a magical place flourishing within your soul.

Because of the size of this project, we may have left out the names of some people who contributed along the way. If so, we are sorry, but please know that we really do appreciate you very much.

We are truly grateful and love you all!

Introduction

Like a bouquet of fresh spring flowers, *Chicken Soup for the Girlfriend's Soul* is sure to soothe the senses and delight the mind's eye. The unique fragrance of feminine friendship pervades each story, carefully handpicked by the editors and a national readers' panel. The resulting arrangement is a profusion of color that captures significant moments from all walks of the garden of life.

In this book you'll discover seeds of familiarity, like simple acts of kindness first sown in childhood that have grown into heartwarming memories. You'll find evidence of the enduring roots of lifelong friendships that can withstand even the harshest storm.

Friendship blooms in all life phases and in some unexpected places—among classmates and professional colleagues, between the young and the young-at-heart, in backyards and boardrooms, at sleepovers and in shopping malls. It can blossom in the midst of a women's group or even in the huddle of a mother and daughter at the kitchen table, where family love triumphs over life's problems and challenges.

The stories in *Chicken Soup for the Girlfriend's Soul* are like fertile soil, rich in relationships and life lessons of love and kindness. They tell how girlfriends help each other through good times and bad. They are there for marriages and breakups, illness and well-being, triumphs and losses. They turn every day into a celebration. They are a listening ear, a kind voice, strength when it is most needed.

These stories teach us not only to cherish and nurture the friendships we have, but even more, to realize that we have an awesome power: With a kind word or gesture, we can reach out so that we are no longer strangers, but attentive witnesses of those miraculous first buds of friendship.

Enjoy!

Share with Us

We would love to hear your reactions to the stories in this book. Please let us know what your favorite stories were and how they affected you.

We also invite you to send us stories you would like to see published in future editions of *Chicken Soup for the Soul*. Please send submissions to:

www.chickensoup.com
Chicken Soup for the Soul
P.O. Box 30880
Santa Barbara, CA 93130
fax: 805-563-2945

You can also access e-mail or find a current list of planned books at the *Chicken Soup for the Soul* Web site at *www.chickensoup.com*. Find out about our Internet service at *www.clubchickensoup.com*.

We hope you enjoy reading this book as much as we enjoyed compiling, editing and writing it.

1

THE TRUE MEANING OF FRIENDSHIP

A friend drops their plans when you're in trouble, shares joy in your accomplishments, feels sad when you're in pain. A friend encourages your dreams and offers advice—but when you don't follow it, they still respect and love you.

Doris W. Helmering

Toasting Rye Bread

A constant friend is a thing rare and hard to find.

Plutarch

I have heard that memory is 80 percent smell. I don't know if that is a verifiable percentage, but every time I put a piece of rye bread in the toaster, I think of Laurie.

I was twelve years old when I discovered that toast didn't have to be made from white bread. I was sleeping over at my best friend Laurie's house when I first smelled the sharp, singed-caraway aroma of rye toast. I was astonished and laughed at her outrageousness: She was toasting rye bread. Then she made me taste it, and I was hooked. This morning, munching on my rye toast, I realized that this was only one small way my best friend had broadened my horizons and that that's one of the things best friends do best.

Aristotle's definition of friendship is the image of one soul dwelling in two bodies. Certainly, that was Laurie and me. Our friendship existed in the pre-menstruation, pre-boyfriends, pre-rebellion pocket of childhood. We were on the verge of everything. Our relationship turned out to be excellent preparation for marriage. It was as consuming as monogamy. We spent every free moment together. We were in the same class. We demanded to know each other's innermost thoughts. We finished each other's sentences. We had the same passions. We argued vehemently, and just as vehemently stuck together. We had little room in our hearts for other acquaintances who didn't know our codes.

Our friendship began when we were the only two new kids in the third grade of a closely knit Catholic school. We sat together in the lunchroom, eight-year-old victims of ostracism, and our segregation soon turned to camaraderie. We were inseparable for five years, until my parents unfeelingly decided to move. Our friendship has lasted through subsequent moves, soul searches, college degrees, fads and grown-up adventures.

For many years, our actual communication has been sporadic. Laurie wrote when her father died, instinctively reaching out. I sent her a wedding invitation and an announcement for each new baby; she answered about every five years. Her return address has always been a surprise, leading to the many cross-outs that eclectic friends make in an address book. Laurie has been a poet, a reporter, an artist in Mexico, a forest ranger in remote areas. She used to criticize my dreams of romance as too mundane. "I know you want a white picket fence," she would chide me. I often felt like a potted geranium in a window box next to her rambling wild rose. But I also always knew she loved me for who I was.

I have thought of her more and more over the years, although our contact has grown less frequent. I now watch my four daughters grow and blossom into their own kinds of flowers, and I remember Laurie. I hear them coordinating outfits, hashing it out about other girls, angling for more time together, picking apart their appearance, their goals, their plans, their parents, each other—attempting to distill their own exact essences, just as Laurie and I once did.

Sometimes I think I am not really old enough to be on the other side of all this. I tell my girls we had no VCRs, that we had to go to the theater to see a movie, and they ask facetiously, "Did you have electricity?"

Yet my sometimes cloudy, sometimes lovely, sometimes fierce memories of childhood are really all I have to draw on as I try to raise my daughters to be kind, honest and full of heart. All the parenting books on my shelf cannot evoke the tug of a best friend "breaking up" with you or the delight of the intimacy of a day at the lake that you wish would never end.

Best friends beckon us to come out from the shadow of our moms and dads. They show us we have separate lives. They offer us affection solely for who we are, surprise us with the scope of another's existence, and teach us it's okay for toast not to be white bread.

My most recent letter from Laurie said that she'd left the Forest Service, gained a husband and was living in Portland, Oregon, in a cedar house they called their "urban cabin." Last summer, we met for the first time in twenty-two years. In the area to visit relatives, our family went to their cabin for dinner. We introduced husbands and children, and reintroduced ourselves. We talked and laughed and caught up on the years that seemed to have flown by. As I described the insight our childhood friendship had afforded me into the lives of my daughters, I realized they gained something from us now as they watched twenty-two years—twice their lives or more—melt away. Two old friends embraced, shared photos, got to know husbands and children. My girls saw firsthand the living truth of *Anne of Green Gables* "kindred spirits" and glimpsed their mother as a girl.

To my daughters, Laurie and I are old. They barely see the point of being almost forty. But someday, all this may filter back through their memories, perhaps as they raise daughters who have best friends and recall their own childhood best friends.

My head is full of cycles; my heart is full of love for every turn.

Valerie Schultz

Nancy and Caroline

Friends are people who help you be more your-self, more the person you are intended to be.

Merle Shain

I came upon the photograph during a recent purge of the old secretary-style desk in the den. It was yellowed with age and almost terminally bent, but if I looked hard enough, I could still make out the figures of two little girls, arms wrapped around one another, smiling into the camera.

What a flood of memories that old photograph brought!

It was from twenty-four years ago when the subjects, our youngest daughter, Nancy, and Caroline, the beautiful child with the shiny brown hair and the enormous brown eyes, were eight years old.

They were best friends. Absolutely bound to each other.

Nancy and Caroline had found one another back in the carpentry corner at nursery school, and had never let go.

No traditional role-playing for these tiny feminists who preferred driving stubby little nails into little slabs of wood to dressing Barbie dolls. It was a friendship that was meant to be.

By the second grade, Nancy and Caroline had become a notorious twosome. Bonded. Attached at the soul.

"I'm going to separate you girls," their long-suffering teacher threatened almost daily. But she, too, saw something so touching—so fierce—about their loyalty to each other that she never could do it.

But in third grade, they were plunked down in different classrooms. Bereft at first, they had railed at the Fates. But they had still managed to find each other whenever they could—at recess, in the lunch line, on the school bus.

"Save me a seat!" never needed to be said. Not between best friends.

So they had played double Dutch until their feet blistered. And they had walked uptown for double-dip ice creams on Saturday afternoons. Then, they had weathered the storms of blemishes and training bras, bewildering bodies and boys, and parents who didn't understand them anymore. Through it all, they had each other, relied on each other.

And they had thought it would last forever.

Until one day, in a voice choked with sobs, Caroline had said the unthinkable: "I'm moving."

Moving. The word made no sense to either of them.

"Not fair!" our Nancy lamented. "Not one bit fair!"

"I'm not going," Caroline had said darkly.

And there were desperate phone conversations and whispered plans that both girls knew would never come to pass. Dramatic value aside, there was no way that these two could halt destiny.

Sure enough, one miserable day the for-sale sign went up on the lawn of Caroline's house. And too soon, too heart-stoppingly soon, the sold sign was plastered over it, and there was a moving truck in her driveway. In a blink, three burly movers were carrying out the kitchen table, the den sofa and the stuffed animals that two little girls had cuddled on the long, precipitous journey from childhood to adolescence.

People were too busy that day to really notice two fourteen-year-old girls in matching jeans, standing together in the gathering dusk trying to figure out how to say good-bye to each other.

But when I looked at that fading picture of Nancy and Caroline, snapped so long ago, I remembered another image, this one of two girls standing on the lawn of a house with a sold sign, tears streaming unashamedly down their cheeks.

On that day, two of tender age were learning one of life's most enduring lessons: There's never another best friend quite like your first.

Sally Friedman

I Found My Best Friend After Forty Years

*There are three things that grow more precious
with age: old wood to burn, old books to read
and old friends to enjoy.*

Henry Ford

Joyce Duffey and I grew up in a small Arizona mining
town during the 1930s and 1940s. She was my best friend
and the sister I never had. When we weren't watching
Shirley Temple movies at the theater, we were taking
piano and dancing lessons. After swims at the city pool in
the summer, we'd split an ice-cold Popsicle down the
middle. At my house, we'd play with dolls for hours on
end and sneak cookie dough my mother had left in the
refrigerator. I went horseback riding with Joyce and her
dad, and she came on my family's picnics. Joyce's mother
had died when she was six, so when we reached adolescence, we both learned the facts of life from my mother.
And together, we discovered what was really important:
makeup, hairstyles and clothes!

So it was difficult for us to part in 1944, when my family

moved 350 miles away. Wartime gas rationing made travel unlikely, and we could only write letters from the time we were separated, at fourteen, through our college years—until we finally were reunited at my wedding, when Joyce, of course, was one of my bridesmaids. After her own marriage, I saw her one more time, when I went to California in the 1950s for my grandmother's funeral.

I never dreamed I would lose touch with her completely. But we both had small children and were so busy with our growing families and many moves across the country that we let our letter-writing lapse. Finally, a Christmas card I sent to Joyce was returned with "address unknown" stamped across the envelope. Her father, too, had died by then, and I had no idea how to find her.

My family and I eventually settled back in Arizona, and as the years went by, I thought of Joyce often. I wanted to share with her my joy and pride as my children grew up, married and made me a grandmother. And I needed, so much, to share my sorrow when I had to put my mother in a nursing home and when first my brother, and then my father, died. Those milestones made me aware of the importance of old ties—and the gap in my heart that only a friend like Joyce could fill.

One day, as I sat reading the newspaper in the spring of 1992, I saw an article about teenage gangs. Next to it was the photo of a social worker named Kevin Starrs. *That's a coincidence,* I thought. Joyce's married name was Starrs, and her husband was a social worker. The young man in the photo did resemble Joyce and her dad. Then I chided myself for jumping to conclusions: *There must be thousands of people named Starrs.* Still, I decided it wouldn't hurt to write Kevin a letter, telling him about my childhood friend and how those coincidences compelled me to contact him.

He phoned me the minute he heard from me. "Mrs. Conder," he said, "Joyce Duffey Starrs is my mother!" I must have yelled loudly enough to be heard in South Dakota—where, Kevin told me, Joyce was living. He was as excited as I was, and I could hear in his voice his love for his mother. After he gave me her phone number and I gave him mine, he added, "You know, three of us children live nearby. My mother visited us here in Phoenix several months ago."

My eyes welled up with tears. "She was here—only a few miles from me—and I didn't even know it?"

I promised Kevin I'd call Joyce that very evening. I didn't have to wait that long. Ten minutes later my phone rang.

"Margie?" Even after forty years, I recognized the voice instantly. As soon as Kevin had hung up from our conversation, he'd called his sister, who'd telephoned their mother and gave her my number.

We laughed and cried, and got caught up on each other's lives. It turned out that Joyce had lived in northern Arizona—so close to me—for a number of the years when we each thought we would never hear from the other again. In the weeks that followed, we talked frequently on the phone and exchanged long letters with photos of our spouses, our children, our grandchildren and ourselves. There were so many things to tell each other!

That summer Joyce flew to Phoenix. When she called me from her daughter's home, I hurried there, excited and nervous. *Would we have that same feeling, that bond, we'd had as children?* But there was no need to worry. She was waiting for me at the front door, and I could still see that fourteen-year-old in her sweet grin.

"You look just the same!" we said simultaneously, as if we both were blind to wrinkles, added pounds and gray hair. We fell into each other's arms.

The next week was filled with hours of catching up, reminiscing and sharing confidences. We giggled like little girls as we pored over old photos. Together, we revisited our hometown, which now looked so small, and other favorite spots where we'd spent time together. The best part of our reunion, though, was meeting each other's children and grandchildren. Joyce had an emotional reunion at the nursing home with my mother, who, though she can no longer speak, smiled with such happiness that we knew she recognized my long-lost playmate.

The empty place I'd had in my heart for forty years has been filled to overflowing with our renewed friendship. Old friends really are the best friends. And there's one more thing Joyce and I now know for sure: We won't lose each other again!

Marjorie Conder

The Friends Who Saved Me

Fortify yourself with a flock of friends! You can select them at random, write to one, dine with one, visit one, or take your problems to one. There is always at least one who will understand, inspire, and give you the lift you need at the time.

George Matthew Adams

Whether it's birthdays and weddings, or break-ups and make-ups, our friends are there to applaud what we do, offer advice, lend support. But what if it's helping someone survive the most agonizing experience imaginable? I can honestly say that if it weren't for my friends, I'm not sure I would be here.

Two years ago, I was driving my three-year-old daughter, Hanna, to her first day of preschool in Princeton, New Jersey, when the radio announcer said: "A plane has just struck one of the World Trade Center towers." Not believing what I'd heard, I walked Hanna to her classroom.

I was back in my car with my one-year-old son, Harris,

getting ready to leave, when the news broke about a second plane hitting the World Trade Center. That's when panic flooded through me—my husband, Steven, worked in Tower One.

A minute later, my cell phone rang. It was my close friend Jennifer, whom I'd met in our kids' playgroup a few years earlier. "I don't think I can drive," I told her.

"Stay put," Jennifer said. "I'm on my way." Within minutes, she was in the parking lot, ready to drive me home. My other friends from the playgroup, Maureen and Lori, rushed to my house. The three of them were practically lying on top of me as we watched Tower One fall on television, and I screamed my husband's name.

None of them knew what to say to me on that day or the days that followed. But they instinctively knew what to do. When I needed to be hugged, they hugged me. When I needed to be left alone, they gave me space. They were going to do whatever it took to make sure my children and I got through this.

I relied on my family too. On September 11, all planes were grounded, so my mother and brother drove, without stopping, to my side—my mother from Chicago, and my brother from Virginia. Mom stayed for weeks.

But my friends were there for me in ways I couldn't have imagined. They created a rotation schedule so that someone could lie with me at night until I fell asleep. Meals were delivered to my home daily. Toys and clothing for the kids poured in. My neighbor, Jean, baby-sat every Wednesday night so I could go to a support group. I relied on these women to help me through some unbearable moments, and they came through every time.

One of the hardest days of all was October 11, 2001. Two police officers rang my doorbell. "Is there someone who could watch your children for a while?" one of them asked. My entire body shook violently when they told me that Steven's body had been positively identified through dental records. Once again, within minutes, Jennifer, Maureen and Lori were at my side.

"He's never coming home," I told them. It was all so real, so final. As the officers told us where the body was being sent, I looked at Maureen and said, "I need to go be with him." She drove me there and held me tightly as we looked at the pine box that was my husband's casket. Together we removed the American flag draped over it, and she helped me rub my tears into the wood so that part of me would always be with him. I am so thankful I did not have to endure that experience alone.

I always knew I had great friends in my inner circle, but what surprised me was how people I barely knew played such a crucial part in my recovery. I met my friend Haidee just one week before Steven's death. After learning that our daughters would be in the same nursery school class, we arranged a playdate for the girls. She never met my husband, nor did she know much about me. So when my doorbell rang a few days after September 11, I was shocked to see Haidee standing there. All she said was, "Can I please come in and sit with you?" Since that day, she and her husband, Sean, have welcomed my children and me into their lives. I can't imagine life without Haidee.

Late last year I turned thirty-five. I had always teased Steven that he'd better throw me a surprise party for this milestone or he'd be in big trouble. Obviously, I had to make new plans. So when Jennifer, Maureen, Lori and Haidee said they'd treat me to lunch and a day at a spa, I agreed. Minutes after I walked into the restaurant, fifty people appeared, yelling, "Surprise!" I was overwhelmed. Never wanting me to feel anything less than special, my friends tried to fill in the gaps left by Steven's death.

I treasured my friends beyond words. Still, my relationships with them did change. Suddenly, I was the only single parent among a group of happily married people. Social gatherings I used to love were transformed into painful reminders of my loss. Friends were reluctant to discuss their marriage problems or even joke about their husbands' silly habits, for fear of making me uncomfortable. At the same time, I often shied away from sharing my innermost feelings with them.

It was at the 9/11 support group that I met Lisa, another widow with young children, who became a great source of comfort. Although she and I came from very different backgrounds and upbringings, we were sisters in grief.

On one particularly bad day, I drove to her house and we sat in her kitchen, weeping about all the things we couldn't say to other people. The unbearable loneliness, the fear, the heavy responsibility of raising children alone—she was going through it all, too. It was such a relief to be with someone who completely understood.

One evening, I told Lisa I was thinking of taking off my wedding band and replacing it with a new ring. It was time to face reality—I was a single, independent woman. I had to start anew. Lisa agreed. But it was a big step for both of us, and we made plans to shop for rings together.

A week later, I was standing outside a jewelry store, waiting for Lisa. When she finally arrived, I got into her car and sobbed: "I remember when Steven gave me this ring, I thought I'd never take it off." She began to cry, as well, and we shared stories of how we got engaged.

"We don't have to do this," Lisa said.

"Yes, we do, we need to do this," I answered.

We went into the store and each bought a ring. Mine is a silver-and-gold cable ring with a chalcedony stone on top. I love it.

These days, I am doing much, much better than I'd imagined I would be two autumns ago. I have grown more confident. My kids are happy, which is the best indicator

I have of how well I've handled things. I talk to them about their father every day.

What I have learned is that being independent is very important, but perhaps even more important is knowing you have people you can depend on. On September 11, 2001, I felt like the unluckiest woman alive. Now, I see how lucky I am, blessed with the greatest friends in the world.

Jill Goldstein
Submitted by Debbie Merkle

Bosom Buddies

With a person I trust I can tell her all my problems without anyone knowing. I can tell her all my secrets like a secret diary.

Priya Patel

The bust cream at $2.98 a jar hadn't worked. My friend Carol and I faithfully read the ads each month in the back of the movie magazines, showing girls with beautiful, fully developed figures. Now that we were almost fifteen, we longed to look just like them.

Scraping together our baby-sitting money, we excitedly sent away for two jars and eagerly awaited the mailman every day throughout June of 1955. We also staked him out because we knew this was not a purchase our mothers would approve of.

Euphoria was ours the day the jars arrived. After the recommended ten applications, like a busted (forgive the pun) balloon, euphoria dissipated into the hot July air. Well, at least for me. Carol was definitely developing, thanks to the cream or Mother Nature (who could say?)

but the proof was there when she put on her bathing suit. She looked so curvy while I, her friend since first grade, was as flat as the tar patches on the hot neighborhood streets.

So one sultry July day, we opted for Plan B. Walking up to our local dime store, we made the second most important purchase of my teen life: falsies. These foam rubber answers to voluptuousness cost $1.98 a pair. Once again, a purchase to be made not with your mother, but only your best friend.

While I went to the ladies department, Carol stood guard in the aisles, lest my mom or one of her friends should come along. We had agreed upon a signal. Three coughs and the coast was clear, two coughs and trouble was near. Hearing the reassuring sound of three coughs, I handed the clerk my purchase. But wait a minute! What was that she was saying? She was out of bags and would be right back? Leaving the falsies right there on the counter in broad daylight?!

Oh, God, no! Please don't let this be happening, my young heart prayed.

Not only was it happening, but so, too, was the unmistakable sound of two coughs. Trouble, real trouble was at hand in the form of Mrs. McDoover, the neighborhood gossip, coming down the aisle. Right there and then, I promised God I'd be a missionary in China if he'd just let that salesclerk return with the bags lickety-split. And she did. Hallelujah!

Carol and I hurried home clutching the bag that held my soon-to-be new figure, well, at least the top portion of it. Once in the bedroom, I tried on my bathing suit with the falsies in place. Oh! It was so exciting! Carol assured me I looked like Marilyn Monroe or even Jane Russell. Well, maybe not that gorgeous, but very womanly, indeed.

What with the ninety-degree heat outside and no

air-conditioning inside, we were sweating up a storm. Hurriedly, we left for the park swimming pool. As luck would have it, this was girls' day.

We dove into the cool water and how wonderful it felt! We swam and swam, until out of the corner of my eye, I noticed something floating by. *Oh, God, no! It couldn't be!* Alas, it was. One lone falsie floating by without a care in the world or a matching partner, for that matter. Right then and there I knew I'd have to stay in the pool until midnight, but then I'd be late for supper, as well as grounded. Embarrassed beyond belief, I climbed out of the pool, ran into the girls' locker room and changed back into my clothes. Carol came in a few minutes later, carrying the falsie in her hand. We walked home, feeling depleted by the entire experience.

The house was sweltering, the six-inch fan blowing hot air on Mom as she sat peeling potatoes for that night's supper of potato salad and cold cuts. One look at my face and she knew the world had ended. Well, at least my little corner of it. Through tears, sobs and hiccups, the shame-faced tale was told. Reaching across the kitchen table Mom took my hand and said, "Go get my sewing basket and we'll fix things right."

That afternoon, over hot tears and cool lemonade, Carol and I learned that the quick answers the world offered to problems were often false, but love that was shared around the kitchen table was often the truest love of all.

Alice Collins

The Swing

Many people will walk in and out of your life. But only true friends will leave footprints in your heart.

Eleanor Roosevelt

Meg, Katie and I sat rocking on the swing on Meg's front porch. Because Katie had the longest legs, it was her job to keep us moving with a gentle push every now and then. Today, our swinging was sporadic. Katie was caught up in Meg's description of the heart surgery she would undergo in two days.

"The doctors say now is the best time," Meg explained. "I've grown all I'm going to, I'm healthy and they don't want to wait any longer. The walls of my aorta are weakening every day."

Katie and I listened quietly. We'd always known that one day Meg would have heart surgery, but we weren't prepared for it to happen this summer. We were having too much fun.

Katie and I had always known Meg was different. She

often complained about the way her eyes protruded from her head and about the extra-thick glasses she wore. We teased her about her slightly bucked front teeth, lovingly calling her "Bugs" after Bugs Bunny. But we never teased her about her heart condition. Meg's family had known from her birth that one day she would require an operation. Now, the day had come.

Meg went shopping with her mom the next day, so Katie and I didn't see her until late. We sat on the porch swing, each of us lost in our own thoughts. When Meg's dad called her in, I hugged her tightly. "I'll be praying for you," I said.

"Thanks," she replied with a smile. "Pray for the doctors, too." We all laughed. Meg's remark had broken the tension.

I didn't sleep very well that night, so it was late when I got up the next morning. I went outside for some fresh air and looked down the row of houses to Meg's. I saw her dad and brother with their arms around each other.

They're home early, I thought. I went in the house just as the phone rang. It was Katie.

"Teresa, I have terrible news."

I could tell she was crying. My heart sank.

"Meg died," Katie said flatly. "When the doctors touched her aorta, it was so weakened, it just dissolved. She died on the operating table."

I was in shock. "Katie, I'll talk to you later," I said, and hung up the phone. As I headed for my room, I passed my mom in the hall.

"Any news on Meg?" she asked.

I shook my head, still too stunned to tell anyone the news. I didn't want to believe it. I shut my door and lay down on my bed.

It can't be true, I told myself. *Meg can't be dead. Katie heard wrong. It was some other girl who died. Meg will call and tell me everything's okay.*

As the hours stretched on, I knew Katie was right—but I couldn't admit it. I heard Katie's mom call mine to tell her the news. When my mom knocked on my door, I told her to go away. "I want to be alone," I pleaded.

On the way to the funeral home, I kept telling myself that Meg was okay. But when I walked into the room with my parents and saw Meg lying there, reality hit. My friend was dead. I walked over to the casket and looked at Meg's peaceful face. She looked like she could jump up any minute and ask why everyone was so sad, but she didn't. Meg was dead.

I cried hot, angry tears. I couldn't understand why Meg had died, and I was mad at God for allowing it to happen. *The world is full of horrible people. Why didn't you take one of them? Why did you have to take the sweetest, kindest person I know?*

God didn't give me any easy answers. At Meg's funeral, her pastor read John 3:16: "For God so loved the world that he gave his only begotten son, that whoever believes in him shall not perish, but have eternal life."

I knew Meg was a Christian, and I was comforted by the fact that she was promised eternal life. As the days passed, I drew on God's promises for those who believe in him. Jesus told his disciples that he was going to prepare a place for them in heaven. I knew that included a mansion for Meg. I missed Meg terribly, but I could feel my anger lessening.

One evening several weeks later, Katie and I were walking when we found ourselves heading for Meg's front porch. We sat on the swing, both uncomfortably aware of the space between us.

"I miss Meg," Katie said as she gave a push.

"Me, too," I replied placing my hand on the empty seat.

"But you know," I told Katie with a smile, "Bugs will have perfect teeth in heaven."

Katie laughed. "You're right, and she can't complain about her eyes or her thick glasses anymore!"

"And no heart defect . . ."

The front door opened and Meg's mom came out. "I thought I heard someone," she said. "I was hoping you girls would stop by. Please keep using the porch swing. Meg's dad put it up for the three of you, and we hate to see it empty."

"We'll be back," we promised.

"No heart defect," Katie said with wonder, as our swinging resumed.

We scooted together, closing the space that had separated us. "Do you suppose there are porch swings in heaven?" Katie asked.

"I'm sure of it," I said firmly. "And I'm sure Meg will be saving us a place on one when we get there."

Teresa Cleary

Power of Love

Proximity was their support; like walls after an earthquake they could fall no further for they had fallen against each other.

Elizabeth Bowen

"Mom! Will you puh-leeze tell Kristen to stop hogging the bathroom?" thirteen-year-old Natasha calls downstairs to her mom, Michele.

"I was in here first!" Kristen, twelve, shouts.

"You girls work it out yourselves!" Michele calls from the kitchen, and sure enough, a few minutes later when Kristen and Natasha troop downstairs with their schoolbooks, they're laughing and gossiping like . . . *Just like sisters,* Michele marvels, and for the thousandth time she thinks, *It's no wonder God put Kristen in my backyard all those times. He knew all along that one day she'd need a new home and family.*

It was seven years before, the afternoon Natasha first pointed out the shy little girl in the Manchester, New Hampshire, schoolyard and said, "That's Kristen. She lives on the street behind us, and her dad's a fireman, just like Daddy."

Natasha was a year ahead of Kristen, but the girls became fast friends. Nearly every afternoon, when Michele looked out her kitchen window, she'd see them climbing trees together or playing on the backyard swings.

"Mom, can Kristen sleep over?" Natasha asked one Saturday, and when Michele called to check with Kristen's mom, Nancy, she was surprised to learn that growing up they'd gone to the same school—just like their daughters.

"I know her husband, Dave Anderson," Michele's own husband, Al, said that night as he set up the rollaway cot in Natasha's room. "He's stationed at Engine Company 11. He's very dedicated."

Kristen and Natasha grew inseparable. They played dolls and did their homework together at Michele's kitchen table. They rode their bikes to Natasha's Uncle Bill's gas station a few blocks away to fill their tires, and from there it was a short ride to her grandparents' house for big bowls of chocolate ice cream.

"Thank you for letting Kristen sleep over again," Nancy told Michele one evening. "My asthma's acting up, and my inhaler isn't helping at all."

"Kristen is always welcome in our home," Michele said. "We all enjoy having her around."

Kristen also enjoyed spending time with Natasha's family. "Wheeee!" she shouted when Al gave the girls rides on their ATV. In the winter, Michele taught Kristen how to ice skate, while Natasha's teenage brothers, Matthew and Nicholas, showed her how to ice fish and swoop downhill on a sled.

But one afternoon Kristen raced through the alley gate, her eyes wide with worry. "Mommy had a real bad asthma attack and Daddy had to take her to the hospital!" she exclaimed.

"I'm sure she'll be okay," Michele comforted her. But that night Nancy suffered a massive coronary, and by morning, she'd slipped into an irreversible coma.

For the next two days, Michele cooked Kristen's favorite meals, like macaroni and cheese, and played countless games of rummy to help keep her mind off her mom. On the third morning, there was a call from the hospital.

"Sweetie, your mom has gone to live with God," Michele told Kristen. When Kristen burst into tears, Michele held her in her arms, feeling thoroughly inadequate.

At a time like this a girl really needs her mom, she thought. *Only now, Kristen will never, ever have a mom again.*

When Michele offered to help with the funeral arrangements, Dave couldn't thank her enough. "I don't know how I'm going to raise Kristen alone," he worried.

"You won't have to," Michele assured him. "We love Kristen. She's always welcome in our home."

Dave tried his best to carry on without his wife, but his grief was overwhelming. Michele sensed Kristen needed a stronger shoulder to lean on, so she enrolled Kristen in a bereavement group and went with her to every meeting. She checked Kristen's homework and attended her class open houses whenever her dad couldn't make it because he was on duty at the firehouse.

Kristen spent the summer swimming and boating with Natasha, Nicholas and Matthew at the lake, and in the fall, Michele threw her a seventh birthday party with a big cake and lots of presents. Kristen's dad, aunts and uncles were all there, and she had a wonderful day. But Kristen's heart was heavy.

"I miss my mom," she told Michele that night as she climbed into the rollaway bed alongside Natasha's. Outside, a thunderclap rumbled in the skies—frightening the girls but leaving a smile on Michele's face.

"That was your mom saying hi," she explained. "And just listen to that rain. Your mom's helping God make the plants grow. She wants you to know she's always around, always watching over you."

Kristen loved helping her dad cook up a big pot of firehouse chili, but Dave worked long hours, and he was still shattered by his loss. "It helps knowing Kristen is in such good hands," he told Michele.

"The heart always has room to love another," Michele assured him.

As the months passed, Kristen became such a frequent houseguest that, when Matthew left home to take his own apartment, Michele and Al moved the girls into his larger bedroom and bought a second bed and dresser just for Kristen.

"We can put your mom's picture and her jewelry box right here on top," Michele said, and Kristen felt so lucky to have a family who loved her and wanted to make her happy.

Natasha felt lucky, too. "I don't know what I'd do if something ever happened to you," she told her mom.

"I'm very proud of you," Michele told her. "Not every little girl would be so willing to share her room, her toys and her family."

Then, one afternoon, Al came home with a grim look on his face. "Something terrible has happened," he quietly announced, sitting on the sofa beside Kristen. "Your dad had a heart attack saving a little boy from a fire," he told her. "I'm so sorry. He's gone to be with your mom."

Kristen was devastated. "Why did God have to take both my mommy and daddy?" she sobbed.

"Sometimes, bad things happen again and again, and we never understand why," Michele said, holding Kristen in her arms and wishing there was something she could do to ease her pain.

Kristen's aunts and uncles would happily have taken in their orphaned niece, but Kristen had been through so much already that Michele worried about putting her through even more upheaval.

"She's already a part of our family," she told Al. "She and Natasha are like sisters, and I couldn't love her more if she were my own flesh and blood."

"Maybe Kristen could stay on with us," Al said, and Michele thought this was a wonderful idea. But would Kristen's relatives agree?

"We know how happy she is here," Kristen's Aunt Judy spoke for the family. "We only want what's best for Kristen, and that's being with people she loves and trusts."

The day Michele and Al petitioned for legal custody, they handed the judge a stack of letters from Kristen's relatives, expressing their heartfelt approval and gratitude to the Poulins. "What do you want to do?" the judge asked Kristen.

"I like living with Natasha's family. They give me everything I need," she said, and without hesitation the judge granted the petition.

"Let's go home," Michele told Kristen, and now, it truly was Kristen's home.

Today, Kristen and Natasha still study together at the kitchen table, and they're both honor-roll students. Michele stays busy driving them to soccer practice and gymnastics lessons at the Y. And one day, when Michele went to the mall to collect the girls, Kristen started waving from across the courtyard.

"Hey, Mom! We're over here!" she shouted, and Michele's heart nearly burst with happiness.

Back at the car, the girls fought like sisters over who got to ride up front. But at home, the bathroom wars are over—now that Al has turned Natasha's old bedroom into a huge new bathroom with a vanity and mirror big enough for two teenage girls to share.

Sunday afternoons, Michele and Al take Kristen to the cemetery so she can place flowers on her parents' graves. Michele keeps a picture of Nancy and Dave on top of the TV with photos of the rest of the family, and she collected baby pictures from Kristen's aunts and uncles and put them into an album so Kristen can have them forever.

"I never want Kristen to forget her parents and how much they loved her," she says. "But it feels wonderful, knowing we've become her family, too."

Heather Black

Flowers from Our Garden

A friend is the one who comes in when the world has gone out.

Alban Goodier

I am in my late forties and have two teenage daughters. My life has been difficult but, by the grace of God, I am a survivor.

My girls and I spent much of their childhood in shelters and living on the street. Though we were together six years, I never married the girls' father. He couldn't hold a job. I am a hard worker, but without a college education, the money I earned just wasn't enough to support us. He spent most of my money on hard liquor, and he didn't come home for days at a time.

One day, after he had threatened to kill me (he became violent when he drank), I packed up my girls and our belongings and headed for a better part of town. I figured I would give my girls a good education, even if we had to live on the street.

I managed to find a job as a waitress at a local coffee

shop and I enrolled my girls in a good public school. My job didn't pay enough for rent, so we moved from shelter to shelter. I was nervous about the address, so I got a post office box and used that address for the school paperwork.

No one suspected we were homeless. My girls went to school every day. When the shelter was close enough, we would walk to school. If we had to, we took a bus. My girls were always very presentable, and I often tried to buy them special little gifts. But mostly, the scarce money we had was put away for their futures.

We had made a pact that we would not tell anyone we were homeless because I was sure this fine school wouldn't allow my daughters to remain if they knew about our situation.

One day several years later, my youngest, Leticia, came back to the shelter and told me her friend's mother had invited all three of us over for supper the following evening. I managed to talk the director of the shelter into allowing me to use the kitchen to bake cookies.

The beautiful two-story home we arrived at the following evening was spotless and comfortable. Mary, the mother, was so appreciative of the cookies. We had a wonderful time and I knew I had found a friend.

A few days later, Leticia came home and said that Mary had asked for our phone number so she could call me to get together. Leticia told her we were having trouble with our phones and she would have me call her. I hated that my girls had to lie.

I called Mary, and again we got together at her house. She and I became good friends. I continually told her that I wanted to have her over to our place, but then I would lie and say we were having trouble with the landlord of our apartment building or that something wasn't working (the stove, the air conditioning . . .).

Mary came into the coffee shop one day and asked if I

could spend my break with her. We took a walk. After a few blocks, she stopped at a vacant house, the most adorable little home with a for-rent sign out front.

Mary asked, "Do you like this place?"

"Oh, very much!" I exclaimed. "But it's way out of my league."

"Why don't we call and find out?" Mary wanted to know.

Upset, I told her that the most I could afford was $350 a month. No one would rent a house for that little, especially not *this* house.

The next day, Mary came into the coffee shop with a big grin on her face and a for-rent sign in her hands. She was so excited that she couldn't hold back the news. "I spoke with the owner of that house and guess what? They're renting the place for $350 a month! It couldn't be more perfect for you and the girls."

"That's impossible!" I protested. "Houses rent for three times that much in this neighborhood."

She explained that the owners didn't really need the money. They just needed someone who would appreciate living there and would take special care of it.

A few weeks later, we moved in. We managed to get some furniture from the Salvation Army. Shari, my oldest, took wood shop in school and made us a fine coffee table. We fixed the place up, and I even planted some flowers, which made me feel like I was putting down my roots. I hoped to stay here a long time, raise my girls and always have a place for them to come home to.

But secrets, I've found, don't usually stay secrets.

One month, I had to mail my rent check, but it was during the holidays and I didn't want it to be late so I decided to drop it off at the post office I sent it to every month. While standing in line at the post office, I heard a familiar voice ask for a package from the box where I sent my rent.

I peeked around the line and was shocked to see Mary.

She was thumbing through her mail when I touched her arm. Tears were starting to form in my eyes and I could barely speak. "Mary, is it your house we're living in? Did you do this for us?"

She put her arm around my shoulder and walked me outside. By the time we reached the sidewalk, I was sobbing. I am a very strong woman, and tears don't come easily. I have been through a lot in my life, but no one had ever been so kind.

Mary told me that Leticia had slipped and told her daughter we were homeless. She said she never would have guessed. The girls were always so clean and well-groomed. She and her husband were selling their first home but it was very special to them. They had owned the house for a long time, and it was paid for. They talked about it and decided they wanted to rent the house to us. Mary hadn't wanted me to know because she was afraid I would think it was charity.

I bring Mary fresh flowers every week from our garden, to show her how much she has brightened our lives.

Mary is my Earth Angel, and I want her to know that I appreciate her kindness and generosity, and that I love her.

Shari is graduating from high school this year, and because we were able to save enough money, she is going to college. Without Mary, this would never have been possible.

I thank God for the strength that has helped my daughters and me endure, but thank him no less for the kindness of my dear friend Mary, who truly is my Earth Angel.

Noreen
(Last name withheld by author request.)

The Wonders of Tupperware

And say my glory was I had such friends.

William Butler Yeats

Many years ago, in the far distant past of 1966, Tupperware parties were all the rage. "Stay-at-home" mom was redundant, and practically all of us "kept house" then. These parties gave us a pleasant and acceptable way to go out for the evening, usually leaving the dads to handle the kids' bath-and-bed routine.

We loved actually talking with people older than five, although our conversations mostly centered around those very topics we knew best—kids and housekeeping. While learning the proper way to "burp" a container, we also discussed burping babies. Usually, after about three hours of listening to the demonstrator, playing silly games and filling out our order forms, we would all go home thinking of the wonderful new plastic additions to our already bulging kitchen cabinets. We might not see each other again for a month or so, until someone else decided to host the next "party."

One day, after a Thursday night Tupperware party at the home of my friend Kay, who lived two doors down from me, I was in the backyard hanging out wash (something else we used to do in the olden days, but that's another story). Kay yelled over the back fence that she had some pastries left over, and maybe we should gather up some neighbors and finish them off with coffee later that afternoon. This was an unusual idea in our neighborhood. None of us had lived there very long and we all had little ones who took up a lot of our time, so we just didn't socialize much except for demonstration parties. I told Kay it sounded good to me, and we called everyone who had been there the night before and made plans to meet at my house at two.

Normally, by two in the afternoon, most of us had the kids down for naps, but we decided to forgo the naps just this once and let them play while we ate the pastries and talked. It was raining out, so the little ones had to play in the dining room of my tiny house, out of sight but within hearing distance, while we moms sat talking in the living room. Before we knew it, two hours had gone by, and everyone hurried off to start dinner before the men got home from work. But something interesting had happened during those two hours, something that we all knew we wanted to continue.

We continued to meet for three more years, every Friday afternoon at two, bringing the kids along to scatter toys and grind pretzels into the dining-room rug belonging to that week's hostess. We didn't mind the mess: We were learning that sometimes all mothers lose their cool with their kids and sometimes every loving husband is an unfeeling oaf. We weren't alone in the world, and we weren't monsters. Sometimes we were just overwhelmed by the frustrations of trying to be the best wife and mother we could be. Amazingly, we discovered other women were having the same struggles. And quite often, just talking about it with friends who really understood allowed us to handle things better the next time we felt like throwing in the towel or strangling somebody.

Week by week, my sanity was saved and my marriage was strengthened because I found a safe place to vent my frustrations and learn new ways of coping. We moms learned from each other while we developed wonderful friendships, and our children learned valuable social skills (such as picking up your own pretzel crumbs) from their tagalong playgroup. And all because of a Tupperware party!

That Tupperware—who knew it could preserve so many things?

Carol Bryant

Everybody Needs Someone

People need people and friends need friends
And we all need love for a full life depends
Not on vast riches or great acclaim,
Not on success or on worldly fame
But just in knowing that someone cares
And holds us close in their thoughts and prayers—
For only the knowledge that we're understood
Makes everyday living feel wonderfully good
And we rob ourselves of life's greatest need
When we "lock up our hearts" and fail to heed
The outstretched hand reaching to find
A kindred spirit whose heart and mind
Are lonely and longing to somehow share
Our joys and sorrows and to make us aware
That life's completeness and richness depends
On the things we share with our loved ones and friends.

Helen Steiner Rice

The Tablecloth

Friends are together when they are separated, they are rich when they are poor, strong when they are weak, and a thing even harder to explain—they live on after they have died, so great is the honor that follows them, so vivid the memory, so poignant the sorrow.

Cicero

Last year, my mother, Rose, lost her best friend of fifty years, Rosa, to cancer. Over a lifetime, Mom and Rosa forged a relationship that transcended the two of them, tightly intertwining their families as well. The two women knew and understood each other thoroughly and plainly, and deeply valued each other's company and wisdom.

Their friendship began when they were young brides, inviting each other to barbecues and cocktail parties where they tried out and polished their cooking skills. A few years later, each became pregnant, beginning parallel journeys of motherhood. As the years passed, together they experienced the normal ups and downs of raising a family, providing one another with daily comfort, encouragement and companionship.

When Rosa's cancer was diagnosed, my mother was her greatest cheerleader. Galvanized by fear and a loss of control, Mom organized meals, shuttled Rosa to doctor appointments, ministered to Rosa's husband and grown children, and when possible, translated medical lingo to a bewildered family. My mother, a quintessential helper, gave Rosa and her loved ones much-needed support, gratified to be the scaffolding on which her fragile friend leaned.

Rosa's prognosis was poor from the start, and within a year, she died. As arrangements for the funeral were made, Mom, herself grief-stricken, played a critical role stabilizing Rosa's family and assisting with important decisions. The fact that she was needed was, of course, good therapy as she struggled through her own emotions.

Shortly after Rosa passed away, her bereaved husband, Jean, called my mother on behalf of their daughter, Marsha, who lived out of town. "Rose," he said, "when Marsha was here for the funeral she turned the house upside down looking for a tablecloth she said Rosa had been working on, embroidery or something. I have no idea where it is, and Marsha is devastated about it. I think Rosa was working on it for her. Do you have any idea where she might have put it?"

The next day, my mother, her heart heavy with loss, pulled up in front of her friend's house. Walking into the dining room, fifty years of knowing Rosa's habits her guide, she opened the bottom drawer of the china cabinet, revealing the tablecloth and napkins Marsha was searching for. Unfolding the embroidered cloth, she said to Jean, "I remember Rosa telling me about this cloth before she became sick. She was working on it for Marsha, but it looks like she finished only half of it before she had to give it up. Do you mind if I finish it?"

My mother carried the cloth home and lovingly studied her friend's handiwork. With tears in her eyes but with a sense of renewal, she threaded the embroidery needle tucked into the fabric and began to sew. For days, she embroidered, each stitch fortifying and healing her.

The tablecloth finished and ironed, Mom draped it over her lap, examining the commingling of her stitches with Rosa's, contemplating the weight of their joint effort and thinking how true it is that the whole is much more than the sum of its parts. With great care, she swaddled the cloth in tissue, placed it in a box and mailed it to the daughter of her best friend.

Bohne G. Silber

I've Fallen and I Can't Get Up!

One can never speak enough of the virtues, the dangers, the power of shared laughter.

Elizabeth Bowen

As the editor of a major travel magazine, I receive many interesting invitations to foreign destinations, and when the opportunity presents, I invite my two best friends on the staff to travel with me. Although Linda and Leslie are junior writers working under me, I consider them to be friends as well. Because they were also my gal pals, I included them when the British Tourist Authority invited me to tour England.

Let's face it, I'm a city girl, born and bred, and so are Linda and Leslie. The only lambs we have ever seen are chops on a plate! But here we were in southern England with Leslie as our designated driver (no point in all of us learning to drive on the left!), motoring through miles and miles of rolling green hills and pastures dotted with hundreds of shaggy white sheep.

A veteran tour guide, Brenda Page, sent to us by the

British Tourist Authority, told us more about sheep than we really cared to know.

"What you're seeing are Hampshire sheep," explained Brenda. "At this time of year, their coats get very heavy, and they begin to itch, so they roll on the ground to scratch their backs. Then they're too heavy to get back up. If you see a sheep on her back with her feet in the air, she may appear to be dead, but she isn't. You'll need to go into the pasture and set her back up on her feet."

We looked at each other in dismay.

"Could we practice on a squirrel first?" asked Leslie.

Brenda looked at her witheringly. "When you see a squirrel with its legs up in the air, it is actually dead and no amount of flipping is going to bring it back to life. A sheep, on the other hand, could stay in that position for weeks on end . . . literally!

"Once you turn a sheep over, you can't let go of her right away. You have to wait until her organs slip back into place and her brain settles back in her head again. If you release her too soon, she'll become disoriented and could fall and break a leg."

"Have you ever done such a thing?"

"Oh, many times! I usually lead groups of walkers through the moors, and when we find a sheep upside down, I get one of the stronger men to help me right her, because, of course, she's anxious to break loose."

After a day of touring, we bid farewell to Brenda and started back to our rented cottage.

"Don't look to the left or right," said Leslie. "I'm not prepared to do any sheep-flipping tonight."

"What on earth will we do if we see one?" I asked.

"Maybe we could call the Royal Auto Club," Linda suggested. "Do they have Emergency Sheep Service in Britain?"

Back in our cottage we sat in front of our fireplace, with Linda sprawled out on the couch.

"Linda," said Leslie tentatively, "are you asleep?"

Linda opened one eye. "Don't even *think* about it!"

"Put your hands and feet up in the air. I want to practice Sheep PR."

"Go practice on Phyllis. She's got a heavier coat."

I glowered at the two of them. "Only *one* of you may be going on the next trip!"

Linda looked at Leslie. "I'll flip you for it!"

Phyllis W. Zeno

THE WIZARD OF ID

May Basket

Forgiveness ought to be like a cancelled note— torn in two, and burned up, so that it never can be shown against one.

Henry Ward Beecher

"Hey, do you know what? Today is May Day!" my sister announced. "Do you remember the May Day baskets we used to make with colored paper and paste?"

Childhood memories and warm feelings engulfed me as I recalled that my sisters and I would run around our neighborhood delivering the not-so-perfect baskets brimming with spring flowers. We would place the handmade treasures on a doorstep, knock on the door, then scurry away as fast as our legs could carry us. It was delightful to peer around a bush and watch our friends open their doors and pick up the colorful gift, wondering who had left it out for them.

I distinctly remember the May Day of the year that I was in fifth grade. That year I was faced with a challenge involving one of my dearest friends. She lived right across the road from our family, and we had walked together to school nearly every day since first grade.

Pam was a year older than I, and her interests were starting to change from the interests that we had shared together. A new family had recently moved into our small town, and Pam was spending more and more time at their house. I felt hurt and left out.

When my mother asked me if I was going to take a May Day basket to Pam's house, I responded angrily, "Absolutely not!" My mom stopped what she was doing, knelt down and held me in her arms. She told me not to worry, that I would have many other friends throughout my lifetime.

"But Pam was my very best friend ever," I cried.

Mom smoothed back my hair, wiped away my tears and told me that circumstances change and people change. She explained that one of the greatest things friends can do is to give each other a chance to grow, to change and to develop into all God wants each of them to be. And sometimes, she said, that would mean that friends would choose to spend time with other people.

She went on to say that I needed to forgive Pam for hurting me and that I could express that forgiveness by giving her a May Day basket.

It was a hard decision, but I decided to give Pam a basket. I made an extra special basket of flowers with lots of yellow because that was Pam's favorite color. I asked my two sisters to help me deliver my basket of forgiveness. As we watched from our hiding place, Pam scooped up the flowers, pressed her face into them and said loudly enough for us to hear, "Thank you, Susie, I hoped you wouldn't forget me!"

That day, I made a decision that changed my life: I decided to hold my friends tightly in my heart, but loosely in my expectations of them, allowing them space to grow and to change—with or without me.

Sue Dunigan

Change of Heart

There are people whom one loves immediately and forever. Even to know they are alive in the world with one is quite enough.

Nancy Spain

All her friends were going to the baby shower, but my daughter, Kathy, wouldn't attend because she had a softball practice. Recently, there always seemed to be some reason why Kathy couldn't attend a baby shower. In my heart, I knew that something must be wrong.

Then I learned the sad truth. She and her husband, Kevin, desperately wanted to start a family and were having no luck. It was extremely difficult for them to talk about, and her father and I were sworn to secrecy. They had seen many doctors and undergone numerous tests, and still no reason for the problem had been found. With each new procedure, their hopes would build, only to end again in sad disappointment. They were on an emotional roller-coaster ride.

Next, they traveled to a clinic in Vancouver, British

Columbia, for in vitro fertilization—an expensive process in which a number of embryos from the couple are grown in a laboratory situation. The doctors then choose the healthiest embryos and implant several in the mother. The hope is that at least one will "take," and she will become pregnant. After three failed attempts, Kathy and Kevin became despondent and were ready to give up. And then, out of nowhere, a dim light of hope began to shine.

Carleen had been Kathy's closest friend from the time they entered high school. They had shared everything with each other ever since. She and her husband, Ward, had been there for Kathy and Kevin through all their hopes and disappointments. Carleen was the only friend Kathy confided in, so she experienced this roller-coaster ride right at her side. When Kathy and Kevin returned from Vancouver, disappointed and heartbroken, she looked at her own good fortune and made a decision. She offered herself as a gestational surrogate mother. Kathy was overwhelmed at this unbelievable gesture made out of pure love from her best friend.

Could it be possible? After further medical, and some legal consultation, they realized this might be a real option. But when it came right down to it, would Carleen really be prepared to go through with it? She had a husband and two small daughters and knew she could not make this decision on her own. Her husband, Ward, began to struggle with what might happen. He felt for Kathy and Kevin, but he also cared very much for his wife. He had concerns about the drugs she would have to take, even though he was told they were safe. He feared for her health and emotional well-being after the birth. What if there were complications? Kathy made sure Carleen knew she had the option of changing her mind. There would be no questions asked and no hard feelings.

Still concerned, Ward finally decided to ask his wife to

say no. She was on her way to phone her with his decision, when he suddenly stopped dead in his tracks. In that moment, he realized he might be preventing the only chance Kathy and Kevin would ever have of having a baby of their own. Ward then told Carleen, "Go ahead. I'll be with you all the way."

The planning began. By now, Carleen's parents knew, and Carleen's dad had many of the same concerns as Ward. I understood his concerns—as Kathy's mother, I had my own. I'd never heard of this kind of thing before; it was all new to me. I was worried about the relationships between the four people and how they might be affected in the future. Not wanting to make things any harder for them, I decided to remain silent, and instead, just sent all of them my prayers.

Leaving their two little girls with Carleen's parents, Ward and Carleen accompanied Kathy and Kevin to a fertility center in San Francisco. Those few of us who knew were sworn to secrecy. The two couples had just gone away for a two-week vacation. If this failed, Kathy was not prepared to handle all the talk and questions from well-meaning friends.

At the clinic, the doctors implanted four of Kathy and Kevin's embryos into Carleen, in the hopes that she would become pregnant. To increase their chances, Kathy underwent the same procedure.

The couples returned home hopeful and began the wait to see if either Carleen or Kathy was pregnant. The tension built as the days passed. And then the news finally came. Success! Carleen was carrying a single baby and Kathy was pregnant with twins. We were still sworn to silence, as something might yet go wrong. Seven weeks passed, and all was well. Twelve weeks passed—still all was well. Suddenly, the news was out, and in our small town this big news spread like wildfire. Fourteen weeks, and then crash—Kathy lost her twins. Again, Carleen was there for Kathy. But this time, Kathy knew that Carleen was carrying her baby, and that helped her make it through.

As the gossip made its rounds, I realized what a strong, special person Carleen was. People would ask her, "How can you give up this baby?" She would respond with no hesitation that it wasn't hers to keep. Because Carleen had two daughters, they would add, "What if this is a boy?" Carleen would answer simply, "It still isn't my baby." A local minister, who happened to meet Carleen, said, "This may work if you never see this baby again." Carleen laughed when she told Kathy, saying, "I think it's a pretty sure thing I'll see you and your baby after this!"

There was also enormous support from the community. One day, I heard Carleen's coworker say, "These girls will pull this off without a hitch. They are both so focused." It was true. Carleen paid no attention to the calendar and allowed Kathy to do all the work—just as she would have had to do had she been pregnant. Kathy accompanied Carleen on all her doctor's visits. As the months passed, the entire community began pulling for the two couples. One lady asked me when the baby was due, adding, "This may be Kathy and Kevin's baby, but it is also the whole community's baby!"

The baby was due January 10, 1998. By Christmas, Kevin was so excited, he was walking on clouds. January 10 came and went with no baby. On January 19, the doctor decided to induce labor. Carleen entered the hospital, and Kathy stayed by her side the whole time. Four days later, Carleen gave birth by cesarean section to a healthy baby boy, 9 pounds, 15 ounces! Ten minutes later, Carleen leaned over to Kathy, gave her a big hug and kiss, and whispered, "Thank you for allowing me to do this for you." Kathy was so moved, she burst into tears of gratitude. Kathy and Kevin, along with the entire community, had a new son.

Carleen returned home to her family the following day to recuperate, and Kathy and Kevin took their little boy home a couple of days later. Tears of joy were shed everywhere as the news spread. A baby shower that was planned for a few close friends grew to a hundred! The whole community gave a special gift of appreciation to Carleen and Ward: a weekend at a resort.

What a story Kevin and Kathy have to tell their son when he is old enough to understand. They named him Matthew Edward, Edward after Ward whose change of heart made such a difference in the gift of life one friend gave another.

Jane Milburn

2

GIRLS JUST WANNA HAVE FUN

There is space within sisterhood for likeness and difference, for the subtle differences that challenge and delight; there is space for disappointment—and surprise.

Christine Downing

Operation: Heart Attack

Sisterhood is powerful.

Robin Morgan

Sometimes the benefit of having friends isn't just the relationship, but the life lessons you learn. This was the case with a group of friends I had during my sophomore year of college at Brigham Young University.

There were five of us who formed the little group—four roommates plus one who just fit in. The combination of personalities in our group—Jessica, Julie, Kathryn, Robyn and myself—provided hours of deep conversation, giggling parties and heartfelt confidences. Because we had so much fun together, we didn't make much effort to socialize with many people outside our group. We had group dates together, ate meals together, went shopping together and held silly late-night parties together.

It became a common pastime to sit around on Sunday afternoons and discuss the other people in the apartment complex where we lived. Usually that meant a fairly brutal critique of clothing, dating, personal habits and anything else we could find to joke about or make fun of. Anyone outside of our circle was fair game for a gossip probe.

One lazy afternoon as the conversation waned, Kathryn said, "You know, we really should get to know some of the people who live here. We sit around and make fun of them, but maybe it's because we really don't know them." There was a lukewarm response to the suggestion. What Kathryn was suggesting would require moving outside our comfort zones, and I wasn't sure that any of us wanted that.

Then Robyn chimed in, "Actually, that's not a bad idea. We don't have to try to be everyone's friends, but maybe we could do something nice for everyone. It's hard to not like people you do nice things for." This was sounding more interesting.

"But there are probably two hundred people in this complex—how can we do something for everyone?" I protested.

Jessica jumped in. "I think I have an idea," she said.

Operation: Heart Attack began. We set three rules for this project: We had to do something individual for each person, it had to be carried out and accomplished in absolute secrecy, and it had to require some sacrifice on our parts. Every Sunday, we would gather in the living room and cut out hundreds of construction-paper hearts. Then we would decide which apartments would be "attacked" during the coming week. Each of us would then receive an assignment to find out who lived in a particular apartment and discover some admirable qualities about each tenant. A couple of nights later, we would gather again and review the information. Jessica would carefully write out a note on beautiful heart-shaped stationery for each recipient. Each one listed at least three things that we truly admired about that person. The notes were always signed anonymously with "JADDA," a word made by combining the first initial of our middle names. Plans were then made for Step Two.

Step Two involved breaking up into teams. We would look at our calendars and divide into partnerships based on schedules. On the appointed night, two at a time, we would wake up at 3:00 A.M., dress in dark, heavy clothing, fill a bag with hearts, tape and notes, and be on our way. We would slip over to the chosen door and begin taping paper hearts all over it. Often we had to go hide in a stairwell when the night watchman or a night-owl resident came by. When the door was "attacked," we would carefully place the notes to each tenant right in the middle, sure to be seen. We'd then quickly race back to our apartment for a few more hours of sleep.

This went on for several weeks. Questions began to arise about who the mysterious JADDA was. We often came upon groups of people debating who was responsible for this strange phenomenon. We would pretend to be as stumped as everyone else, then race back to our apartment and applaud our success. Some people even tried staying up late at night to catch us, but we always managed to evade detection. Everyone in the complex seemed friendlier, more interested in each other. Our adventure was bringing consequences none of us had dreamed of.

I noticed the greatest benefit a few weeks after Operation: Heart Attack officially ended. It was a typical Sunday afternoon, and we were sprawled out in the living room discussing the people in our apartment complex. Instead of the rude comments, snickers and criticism that had been the content of previous Sundays, there were concerned inquiries and tones of admiration. As a different person became the topic of conversation, everyone would chime in with the things they liked about him or her. We had become aware of the challenges each of our neighbors faced and were touched by their achievements.

None of our fellow tenants ever knew who was behind Operation: Heart Attack, and we wanted it that way. Everyone in that apartment complex gained their own private cheering section that year. But our favorite reward was the friendship the five of us gained. Where we had been united by common interests and situations in life, we were now united by a powerful experience of learning to love. We've often looked back on that adventure as the bonding experience that sealed our friendship—a bond that has been unbroken as the years have gone by and scattered us across the country. Sometimes, the best lesson we learn from friends is simply how to be one.

Wendy Simmerman

Birthday Presents

I clicked my Palm Pilot and flashing words reminded me that I had not completed a task. Staring at the screen, I worried about what in the world I was going to get Colette for her birthday. After almost thirty years of friendship, I was running out of ideas. And it wasn't just for Colette.

I was blessed to have seven incredible lifelong friendships that began in my childhood. Colette, Marcy, Amy and I became steadfast friends while coloring in kindergarten. We added Mary, Kimmie and Rachel to the group in junior high while chasing boys. Claudette joined us in high school while going to football games. With friendships that spanned decades, together we played jump rope, studied, went to dances, fell in and out of love, graduated, traveled, began careers, really fell in love, married and had children. This colorful group of friends had seen each other at our very best and our very worst. No matter what changed in our lives, one thing stayed the same—our friendships.

Here I was, though, staring at my Palm Pilot realizing I

was going to be really late with Colette's birthday gift if I did not buy her something today. *What could I get her?* Last year was a magazine subscription to *O, the Oprah Magazine,* the year before that Yankee candles, before that Crate and Barrel wineglasses, and before that scrapbook-making kits. Besides, as my friends married and we grew older, we already had just about everything we needed. *What could I buy her?*

The phone rang and I was happy to escape my unsuccessful pondering. Marcy greeted me cheerfully and began to tell me about last night's girls' dinner. Conversations like this always made me miss my childhood home in Illinois and made it hard to live in Washington, D.C., so far from my friends. Marcy filled me in on the latest gossip. Mary was pregnant with child number four and Amy's son Jake was potty-training. Colette would probably be engaged very soon and Marcy was finalizing her wedding plans. On and on we chatted while laughing about the latest happenings in our lives. Finally, I asked Marcy what she was giving Colette for her birthday. Marcy exclaimed, "Oh, I almost forgot to tell you! Last night we were all talking about our birthdays and how hard it is to buy something unique and useful after all these years of friendship. Also, with everyone having kids, school costs, homes, vacations and basically life, we decided that expensive birthday gifts for our friends really add up. So we decided that this year we're giving each other socks." I laughed and said, "What a great idea!" Marcy continued, "No more than two pairs and they can be any kind of socks. You know, those cute little socks with patterns, or trouser socks, or workout socks. Whatever you want. Next year we're all giving underwear! You should have heard that discussion about who wears thongs, granny underwear or lace! It was hilarious. The year after that we're giving earrings. Isn't this fun?" I quickly agreed and kept smiling. We chatted a few more minutes and hung up.

I tossed my Palm Pilot into my purse and headed to the store. While driving, I couldn't help but think about how smart my friends were. It wasn't the physical gift or the amount of money we spent that was important. What was important was celebrating our friends' birthdays. The inexpensive themes allowed us to be clever, and perhaps even funny, yet it would be low stress and useful. As I thought of the years ahead, I smiled because from now on birthday buying was going to be so easy and fun. And when you really think about it, regardless of what's inside when we unwrap each other's presents, what we really unwrap is our love.

Marguerite Murer

That's What Friends Are For

A friend is one who knows all about you and likes you anyway.

Christi Mary Warner

"So how are you enjoying retirement?" asked Crystal at the other end of the long-distance line. Although she lives in Colorado and I live in Florida, I consider her one of my closest friends.

"I've only been retired for two weeks," I protested. "I don't know yet."

"What are you doing to celebrate?"

"I'm having a dinner party Sunday."

"Aha!" said Crystal, the consummate hostess. "What are you serving?"

"I was thinking of onion soup dip and chips for hors d'oeuvres, and since one of the husbands is a vegetarian, I figured vegetarian lasagna for him and meat lasagna for everyone else."

"Wait a minute! You're retired now, and you're going to serve TV dinners?"

"Well, they're my closest friends. They know I can't cook."

"If you can read, you can cook," corrected Crystal. "Hmm, only six, eight with you two, a small party."

"Two more than I have chairs for. I call that a large party."

"Here's a grocery list. When you get all these things in the house, I'll tell you what to do with them."

Dutifully, I wrote down the list she dictated. "I can't thank you enough, Crystal," I said.

"That's what friends are for, darling," she demurred and hung up.

Two full grocery carts later, I was on my way home, ready to start cooking.

The phone rang.

"Hi, lady. I hear you're having a dinner party for your retirement."

"Who's this?"

"Marty in Washington. What are you making for appetizers?"

"I'm thinking."

"You should be like Cher in *Mermaids* and just serve appetizers for the whole meal."

"I don't remember that."

"It was too funny. But here's a great one. Write this down. You buy a loaf of party rye . . ."

She proceeded to tell me the rest of the ingredients. "Thanks a bunch, Marty."

"It's nothing, dear. That's what friends are for."

I was off to the store and back just in time to catch the phone, again.

"Hi, sweetie. Marge here. Do you have a big enough tablecloth for your dinner party?"

"As a matter of fact, I just bought some new place mats.

They're adorable . . . red and white stripes with white stars in a field of blue."

"You bought American flags? You're using American flags for place mats?"

"No, no. Trust me, they're very pretty."

"Well, just remember I'm here for you. That's what friends are for."

I unloaded the groceries and called Crystal to find out what to do with them.

Crystal was in her element. "You start by making a roux. You know how to make a roux, don't you?"

"Mate two kangas?" I asked brightly.

There was a withering silence on the other end of the line; then the phone went dead.

Uh-oh, there went my entrée. Before I could call her back, the phone rang again. She knew I was just joking. But it wasn't Crystal.

"Hi, dear. It's Samantha. I hear you're giving a dinner party."

"Where are you?"

"In London, of course."

"I thought you were upset because you weren't invited."

"Of course not. What are you wearing?"

"Right now?"

"No, at the party, silly."

"An apron probably. I'll be in the kitchen the whole time."

"You need to wear something smashing. You don't want them to think you've become a frump now that you're retired."

"What are you, the fashion police? I have to go back to the grocery store. I forgot parsley. Bye."

It was 5:30 P.M. In twenty-four hours, my guests would arrive. My kitchen was in total chaos, with dips and chips and sour cream and whipping cream and cream cheese and cottage cheese all over the place.

When the phone rang, I had had it. I wouldn't pick it up. But it kept on ringing and finally I gave in.

"Hi, dear. It's Karin. How are you doing?"

"Karin! I'm having a nervous breakdown. Are you calling to tell me you can't come tomorrow night?"

"No, no, of course we're all coming. But we girls just had an idea! You're retired now so why should you work all day to fix dinner for us? Why don't we try that new restaurant? We'll all go dutch. Wouldn't that be more fun?"

"Do you mean it?" I blubbered. "But I couldn't ask you to do that . . ."

"Of course you could. It's all settled. That's what friends are for!"

Phyllis W. Zeno

In Praise of Best Girlfriends

*A friend never defends a husband who gets his
wife an electric skillet for her birthday.*

Erma Bombeck

There are no courses in how to be a best friend, or in
how to find one either. There's no Friends 'R' Us person-
alized dating service you can sign up for. If you're lucky,
you stumble upon a lifelong best friend by accident.

There has to be extraordinary chemistry in a friendship. And by this, I mean Mouth Chemistry. *Motor*
mouth chemistry. Otherwise, all you have is a fond
acquaintanceship.

No man will ever understand this, but the main pre-
requisites for friendship are nonstop talking at the same
time for at least seven and a half hours, followed by going
home and then calling each other up on the phone in
order to discuss all the things that were not discussed in
person. In the case of my best friend, Judith, it is particularly extreme because she is a columnist, like me. We see
each other in person, then we call each other immediately

on the phone, then we write each other letters about the things that weren't discussed in person, then we send each other copies of the column we wrote about the visit and the phone call.

How did I decide that Judith was going to be my friend? It was easy.

When I first visited her home, I saw immediately that she had the same Purina Cat Chow ad taped to her refrigerator that I have taped on mine. This struck me as not merely cosmic but decisive.

Also, her husband is not a jerk. It's amazing how many best friends insist on acquiring wholly unacceptable husbands. If best friends were required to fill out a form before acquiring a husband, the world would be a better place, but so few of them show this kind of courtesy.

So now, let's review the criteria so far: nonstop talking, identical refrigerator art, acceptable (or at least non-jerk) husband. Who could ask for more?

But I have omitted the most important trait of all: generosity.

By this, I do not mean "free with money." Very few women care about that type of stuff. Money was invented by men, and then men invented office buildings so that they could have a place to talk about their money and write amounts of money on pieces of paper and fax them to each other.

When I say "generosity," I mean a generosity of spirit: a lack of pettiness and jealousy, and a meeting (or close to it) of the minds. "This is obvious," you say, but alas, it is hard to find in a friend.

I had a best friend for a while who was a professional therapist. A very nice woman, actually. Unfortunately, therapists and humor columnists do not get along very well.

The first time I saw the therapist's house, I said, "Oh,

what a dump!" (It was actually a gorgeous house, and everyone knew it and said so.) But "Marion" looked at me and said, "Stephanie. You seem a little hostile."

"It was a joke!" I said. Marion looked at me as if I had a frog crawling out of my eye.

Marion and I tried to be friends for a while, but we had radically different philosophies of life. Her philosophy was that I was out of my mind; my philosophy was also that I was out of my mind but that I deserved to be paid for it.

After a while I stopped seeing Marion because I felt she was excessively biased in favor of rational, tasteful behavior.

Luckily, my friend Judith agrees with this, wholeheartedly.

To wit, I recently called Judith up and said, "What's your Thanksgiving column about?"

"It's about liposuction," she said. "It's about how every time I look at jellied cranberry sauce, I think that it must be the stuff that they go in and vacuum out."

"That's disgusting," I said. "Can I steal that idea?"

"Sure," she said.

But the thing is, you see, I lied to my best friend: My column is not about jellied cranberry sauce—it is about her.

And now I have to pencil seven and a half hours into my schedule so that we can talk about it. The screaming alone should take four and a half. I am not sure whose dump we will meet in.

Stephanie Brush

To Pee or Not to Pee

*Friends have come to an agreement. You put up
with my idiosyncracies and I'll put up with
yours.*

Pam Brown

Judy didn't look like she'd be a friend of mine. We
weighed about the same, only she was five inches taller.
All through our adolescence she had boyfriends and later
curfews, cooler part-time jobs (she lied about her age and
was one of those perfume spritzers at a department store
in downtown Brooklyn; I worked checking in dirty clothes
at my father's cleaning store) and great makeup. Judy
excelled at everything I had trouble with—math, Spanish,
standing up for herself and tampon insertion.

After high school we both went to Brooklyn College. We
traveled back and forth together each day and both
graduated with degrees in elementary education. So it
was that on a cold December day, we arranged to take the
necessary physical exam needed before we could be
licensed as teachers—together. We took the subway

downtown to the Board of Education and stood on the long lines, filling out endless forms, one behind the other. It was how I pictured the Army—hundreds of us, single file, going from office to office, doctor to doctor, getting our application stamped.

Midway through the long day, we made a pit stop at the bathroom. We used the facilities, reapplied our lipstick—mine a pale pink, Judy's a hot tangerine—and quickly rejoined our comrades on line.

"A through F, follow me," barked a heavyset woman who looked like she probably moonlighted on the weekends as a warden in the movies.

Perfect. Forman and Finkelstein, we obeyed as she led a group of us back to the bathroom we just left. Then she handed each of us a paper cup.

"I need a urine sample," she growled, "quickly, please. We're on a tight schedule here; don't hold up the works."

Now the last thing in the world I wanted to do was hold up the works. But I had just gone to the bathroom, not five minutes before. No way could I urinate again.

Judy and I sat down in adjoining stalls. Not five seconds later, I heard Judy fulfill her responsibility. That unnerved me even more.

"How do you do that?" I whispered.

"Nothing to it," she giggled. "Let's get out of here. Dragon lady gives me the creeps." Then I heard her flush.

Nothing I had ever admired about Judy—not her thick black hair, her ability to memorize the lyrics to a song after hearing it once, the edge she had over me in sexual experience—rivaled my awe at how she could pee on demand.

"I can't go," I hissed. "How is a person who just emptied her bladder supposed to have enough left for a urine specimen?" I tried to joke but there was nothing funny about how I felt.

"Meet me at the stairwell," boomed the matron. "We're

due at the lab for a blood test in three minutes."

I started to sweat. "Go on without me," I sighed to my friend next door. "I don't want to get you in trouble."

"I'm not leaving here without you. Calm down. There's no problem. I'd donate a kidney if you needed it; don't you think I could spare some urine? Just pass your cup under the stall. I'll divide whatever I have in half."

I did, and she did, and we both emerged from the toilet. We handed our cups to a woman posted at the door.

Relieved, I gave Judy a big hug as we continued onward to the stairwell.

"I'd be happy to return the favor and supply the blood for your test," I said, wishing I could.

Judy smiled. "By the way, don't freak out. There's a chance they're going to notify you that there's some albumin in our urine. It's not a big deal. Between my mother's diabetes and my whatever sex life, it sometimes shows up. Just ignore it."

Albumin? A letter is going to come to my house, the house my father lives in, that says I have albumin in my urine? Albumin that signifies sexual stuff is going on? That my mother will make me go to the gynecologist for? My life was over.

I sweated out the next week. And the next, till the notice arrived with the news that I was indeed a healthy, albumin-free New York City schoolteacher. Someone once said that in real friendship the judgment, the genius, the prudence of each becomes the common property of both. Judy and I experimented with expanding the definition, just a bit.

Marcia Byalick

Half the Fun Is Getting There

A friend is a gift you give yourself.

Robert Louis Stevenson

It never crossed our minds that we were doing something outrageous. Although it was summer vacation, both our husbands had to work. Yet Annette, pregnant and showing, and I, with my hurt knee, decided to take our kids and get away. With five children under the age of seven, we knew our trip would not be lacking adventure.

We packed the van carefully. With sleeping bags, five squirt guns, junk food and the latest chick flick, we headed toward the mountains. Even with "Veggie Tales" playing in the background, it wasn't long until our crew became restless.

"He's touching me!"

"He has to touch you; we're packed in here like sardines."

"How long until we get there?"

"Hey," Annette said in her teacher voice, "half the fun is getting there!"

A couple of hours later, we rounded the mountain and soon stood on the doorsteps of Oakhaven, my parents' mountain home.

"Who's got the key?" one of the kids hollered.

The key! Oh no! In the midst of packing the van, I had set the key down on my kitchen counter. I had forgotten the key. Immediately I said a quick prayer. Then grabbing Annette's arm, I whispered in her ear, "Remember you said half the fun is getting there? Well, we're not inside yet, and the key is at home on my kitchen counter!"

Quickly turning our situation into a game, Annette, the kids and I began rattling all doors and checking all windows for a way inside.

"Look here!" Annette shouted. "The kitchen window above the sink doesn't have a safety lock. Janet, if you hoist me up, I can open the window and crawl through."

"You can what? You're pregnant!"

"Well, you can't do it. You've got a bad knee."

Before I knew it, all five kids stood cheering, watching Annette crawling through the window while I braced her. As Annette's feet disappeared from sight, one of her kids shouted, "Mom, remember that half the fun is getting there!"

We had a great time during our vacation at Oakhaven. The kids laughed, played, hiked and even learned to whistle through an acorn. Annette and I found the time to talk like schoolgirls, and late one night when the kids were tucked in bed, we curled up and watched our chick flick.

Looking back to the days when Annette and I so daringly headed for the mountains with our little brood, we both smile. For now we know for certain that half the fun of motherhood is sharing it with a friend.

Janet Lynn Mitchell

Christine's Comfort Shower

"You're going *where*?" My husband stared at me bug-eyed.

"To Christine's bridal shower," I said, tugging my coat over my flannel pajamas. "It's a comfort theme. I'm supposed to dress this way."

He laughed. "Don't get pulled over."

Langdon, Christine's colleague from the Hand Workshop Art Center, greeted me at the door of Clydie's house. Sporting a baseball shirt, athletic shorts and tube socks, she was the spitting image of me in fifth grade. Right down to the pigtails.

"Love the outfit," I said. "Where should I put my gift?"

"I'll take it. But first you have to put this on." Langdon clipped a bottlecap pin of Christine onto my pajama top. "Now you're a member of the Christine Fan Club," she said.

I laughed and went upstairs to stow my coat. Pit stopping in the hall bathroom, I noted colorful stick figures adorning the commode's outer lid. *How great that Clydie let her kids paint the toilet,* I thought. *I wish I were that flexible.*

Downstairs, I joined other guests milling in the kitchen.

Clydie, clad in a tank top and lounge pants, skittered about, filling wine glasses and pulling food from the oven.

"Hey, Nicole," I said, spying a friend. "It's weird to dress this way, isn't it? I feel like I should be climbing under the covers, not sipping white wine."

"Yeah. But isn't it great? Imagine if we wore jammies every day. It'd be so much more comfortable."

"Deborah . . . good to see you! It's been a while." Jo, the director of the Hand Workshop, strolled over. *She's even polished and professional in sleepwear,* I thought, noting her luxurious silk pajamas and color-coordinated flats. Cushiony carrot slippers cradled my feet. It hadn't even occurred to me to wear something sexy.

Suddenly, laughter tumbled from the front hallway, rousing me from my fashion emergency. Christine greeted friends with warm embraces, and I shuffled along among the well-wishers.

"It's so good to see you," I said finally. "Thanks for including me."

Christine squeezed my hand. "I'm glad you're here."

"Okay, everyone," Clydie yelled over the ruckus. "Let's eat!"

We funneled into the dining room. My eyes popped. *Oh, my gosh! There's more food than at Thanksgiving.*

Nicole held up a fifties-style menu. "Look! The food has special names like Best Man Beans, Eloped Eggplant, No-More-Madajewski Mashed Potatoes. . . ."

"Too funny!" I said, helping myself to Turkey Trousseau and Spousal Stuffing.

After dinner, Langdon directed everyone into the family room. "Big circle, ladies. It's activity time."

We settled in. Langdon continued: "We're going to decorate paper dolls. Your job? Design a bridal outfit. You've got lots of girls to choose from." Langdon flipped through the stack of ten-inch cardboard cutouts. "We've got Lana

Turner, Elizabeth Taylor, Carmen Miranda . . . plus, some modern stars like Buffy and Chandler from *Friends*. He'll make a beautiful bride!"

Laughter erupted.

"And we've got tons of supplies," added Clydie, carting in cardboard boxes. "Tulle, felt, ribbon, lace . . . you name it. Can you tell you're in the home of a Girl Scout troop leader?"

The air was abuzz with creative energy as I plucked Sarah Jessica Parker from the pack and reached for a scrap of white silk. My hand froze. I glimpsed gold and crimson backed by a sea of turquoise. I hesitated, then snatched up the paper napkin. *Why can't I make a tropical bride?* I mused, smiling.

After a champagne toast and gift-giving festivities, Langdon tried to lure us into playing charades. Her attempt fizzled worse than flat soda.

"All right," said Clydie. "No one can leave without playing this last game."

Like a group of obedient schoolchildren, we followed her into the back hallway. Plastered to a door was a glossy photo of a hunky nude male, his private area covered with a bull's-eye.

"It's 'Pin the Manliness on the Man,'" someone wisecracked.

Sure enough, a pile of colorful "parts" lay nearby. Hoots and hollers followed.

"Settle down, ladies," said Langdon, laughing. "Who wants to go first?"

"Oooh, me!" Shelley, a usually reserved watercolorist, muscled her way to the front. Langdon blindfolded her, spun her around, and sent her teetering toward the target.

Meanwhile, a battle raged inside of me. Pre-party Deborah longed to melt into the back of the crowd, but Daring Deborah wanted to spring forward and make my mark on the man. When someone shouted my name and shoved me forward, I was relieved. My face flushed and my head tingled as Langdon sent me groping forward in a world of darkness.

"The quiet ones are always the wildest!" yelled a voice from the back.

Just you wait! Next time, I'll be leading the line. And I won't be wearing flannel!

Deborah Ritz

A Good Connection

If I had a single flower for every time I think of you, I could walk forever in my garden.

Claudia Grandi

Whenever I heard "A-yuh-n," it had to be Karen calling. No one else ever drew my name out to three syllables. Never stopping to identify herself, she just leapt in. I would answer the phone, hear my name elongated and know Karen had something to share.

For two years, hers was the voice that made me stop and sit down. Her soft, slow drawl always held love. Whether the subject was frivolous or fraught with urgency, I reveled in the warmth of that voice. How glad I am now that I treasured those calls.

Not that the conversation was anything but predictable "mommy chat." She'd relate a funny incident that had occurred at the grocery store, commiserate about our pubescent daughters' temperaments or fuss over what type of dog to get for her three rambunctious kids. Nothing earth-shattering, just day-to-day experiences aired and shared.

Then she was gone, snatched away by leukemia, which came out of nowhere and disappeared with her as quickly and mercilessly as it had come.

Her absence was palpable. My hair began to fall out by the brush-full, and unless I stayed constantly on guard, tears overwhelmed me at unpredictable moments—stopped at a traffic light or standing in a warm shower. My dearest friend was gone.

A few years before we met, I was a young professional nearly always in the company of men. The ratio at work was often 1 to 10 in their favor. I aped male-bonding techniques and enjoyed blending in with the guys. Like other ambitious young women in the seventies, I tailored my business dress toward men's styles, and felt that everything worthwhile in life happened outside the home.

We baby-boomer girls, who came of age in the era of Women's Lib, didn't much value housewives and mommies. When I met Karen during my mid-thirties, I'd had no real "girlfriends" since my college days. The birth of my first child didn't change that. Wouldn't it be frivolous to take more than work hours away from my family just to make friends for myself? So when we moved to the suburbs, in the typical city-for-good-schools trade-off, I had plenty of attitude concerning the identity of local mommies.

You're probably way ahead of me here, but I found it a stunning revelation that the "gals" of my narrow-minded stereotype did not exist.

All around me, women were improvising and re-creating the world to suit themselves: women at a variety of life stages and ages, stitching individual patchwork quilts of parenting and life.

The mommies I met turned out to be psychologists, corporate trainers, artists, designers, teachers, office managers, writers, singers, actors . . . and on and on.

They were also alchemists: mixing various proportions

of employment and home, in order to plow huge stores of energy into family and community. On the playground or volunteering at school, I discovered creative, purposeful, powerful women.

Karen had chosen to be a full-time mom during the years we were friends, so it was ironic that she was the one who opened my eyes to the joy of spending time one-on-one with my new peers. A gracious woman who had grown up in rural America, her rhythm was slower than my city-girl pulse. She took time with interactions.

Afternoon phone calls over cups of coffee became a nurturing ritual, which helped me balance the emotional juggling act of job/kids/home.

She gave me license to rehash worries or troubles until solutions were found or at least my spirits were calmed. Better still, she could get me to laugh at myself, just as she laughed at herself. She could even laugh about toilet training.

Try that topic on a male coworker.

Her friendship was a precious gift. My sadness at her death was so deep because I felt I'd lost that gift forever.

I was mistaken. I soon discovered that Karen's gift to me had not simply been her friendship. It was the joy of having women friends. That is a legacy that remains with me.

I rediscovered it in the face of one friend who eased my sorrow when Karen died. I continue to find it in her Fourth of July picnics. It's in another friend's patient smile when our sons get overly adventurous, and another's invitations to join her in political activism.

When my phone rings now, I know in a moment who it is. "Want to hear something funny?" means Kim has a tale to tell; the rising pitch of "Anne?" means Paula has a grin on her face; a clipped "Hi, Anne," means Maria wants to make plans.

They don't need to introduce themselves; their voices

are as much a part of the fabric of my week as Karen's voice is of the fabric of my memory. For them, I stop in my tracks and listen, knowing that they're each giving me their own gifts, for which my life is richer.

Of course, none of them is likely to turn my name back into a multisyllabic wonder. I have Karen to thank for that . . . and also for a lifetime of good connections.

Anne Merle

Reprinted with permission of King Features Syndicate. ©1996 Julie Larson.

Opening Doors

The doors we open and close each day decide the lives we live.

Flora Whittlemore

There are thirty-two pairs of teenage eyes on me, and I'm beginning to sweat. It's Career Day here at Denver's Kennedy High School, and I'm speaking about my job as an international journalist.

So far, my speech hasn't gone too well. The young man in the back corner is asleep, and a girl in the front row is playing games on her cell phone. Most of the others have a glazed look in their eyes.

Desperate, I plunge further into my talk, describing assignments in Thailand, interviews in England and stories in Singapore.

But I may as well be speaking of the moon. For most of these students, the rest of the world is a far-off place. They have little exposure to it, and frankly, they're not all that interested.

And who can blame them? I once felt just as they do.

After all, when you grow up in the middle of a big, powerful country, where exposure to other lands and ways of life are somewhat limited, it can lead you to believe that the rest of the world is just like the one in which you grew up. So what reason is there to explore new places? I had little interest in other countries and cultures.

Then I met Melanie.

We all have people who come into our lives who influence or change us, somehow. For me, one of those people was a twenty-year-old girl from Iowa.

I was attending college in Indiana that year, and I met Melanie on the school's softball team. In truth, we really didn't play much, but sat out game after game with injuries. While our team sailed on to victories without us, Melanie and I sat on the bench and talked. Eventually, we became roommates.

Melanie was different from anyone I had ever known. She made me laugh with her witty sense of humor, but most of all, she was a storyteller. Her tales were different, though, for she had actually been outside the country.

Day after day, she wove stories of places I had never imagined. She talked of dreamy Austrian villages and narrow, ancient streets. She told of tall, handsome Dutch boys and the thrill of cruising down the autobahn.

At first, I feigned disinterest, but eventually, I began to listen, picturing this world that she painted with words. Gradually, like Chinese water torture, Melanie wore me down.

"Okay!" I said one evening after a long story regaling the thrills of travel. "I give up! I want to see this for myself. Let's go!"

And so we did.

Culture shock set in as soon as we set foot in Rotterdam on that weeklong trip during semester break. Surrounded by the staccato sounds of Dutch, I felt like a fish out of water. I wanted to rush back to the plane and head for the familiarity of home.

But I was stuck here, so I followed Melanie through the streets of Rotterdam. She laughed and talked with everyone she met, not afraid of the new things she saw. Slowly, I began to view this new world through her eyes. My discomfort first turned to curiosity, then real interest.

We spent New Year's Eve in Rotterdam, and I watched in awe as the local residents poured into the streets that night, lighting monstrous fireworks, drinking warm drinks and greeting one another (and me!) with two-cheeked kisses.

Right then, even though I couldn't understand a word spoken around me, I smiled with glee. This once strange land that had felt like Mars suddenly turned into heaven on Earth.

From there, Melanie and I rented a little Peugeot and headed out through Europe. We fumbled our way through the countryside, getting lost, but always stopping to ask cute boys for directions. We ran into difficulties with the new languages and cultures, of course, but Melanie just laughed and considered it an adventure.

We drove through Holland and Germany, but it was Austria that stole my heart. The beauty of the Alps surrounding Salzburg took my breath away; and in the cozy cafés that are such an integral part of Austrian culture, I discovered a never-before-seen side of myself. I discovered the quiet joy of sitting all afternoon around a tiny table, drinking dark coffee with whipped cream and discussing the meaning of life with new friends.

Perhaps that is why we are drawn to travel; for leaving our homes and venturing into other parts of the world reveals a side of ourselves that we would never discover otherwise. In learning about others, we learn most about ourselves.

Vienna was the icing on the cake. Wandering with Melanie and my new Austrian friends at midnight down the cobblestone streets of this former imperial city, I could barely contain my delight. Something, I knew, had awakened deep inside of me.

Nine months after that first trek to Europe, I packed up my college boxes and moved to Austria, where I attended university before eventually returning home to the States. My life had turned down a whole new path.

Sadly, that path didn't include Melanie. She graduated and became a teacher. True to her love of adventure, she chose to work in a whole new city and culture: San Antonio, Texas.

My fascination with exploring other cultures and destinations never left me either. I went on to become a journalist, and then an editor for an international travel magazine.

For almost a decade, Melanie and I lost touch. Then one day, a colleague asked me, "Why did you choose this career path?"

In my mind, I immediately saw an image of Melanie, chatting over dinner at the college cafeteria, telling me stories of worlds I had never known. It was time to track down my long-lost friend.

That evening, I looked up Melanie's parents on the Internet and called them. I learned that they were still living in Iowa and that my former roomie had gone on to become a principal, turning around entire schools with her passion for success and achievement. I grinned as I dialed her number.

With some friends, lost years just slip away and you're right back to your same relationship. That was how it was with Melanie and me. Within minutes, she had me laughing as we talked. Life was going well, and my friend was very successful. "But I really miss having the chance to travel," she admitted.

So we remedied that. Every year, we meet up somewhere in the world and spend a week exploring. Last year, it was the Scottish Isles; this year, it will be Switzerland. Who knows where we'll end up after that?

Melanie is the reason I am standing in front of this classroom today. So I stop my speech, take a deep breath and try another angle. Forget stories of journalism; there are better tales to tell.

So I begin to talk of Dutch celebrations, of dreamy Austrian villages and the thrill of cruising down the Autobahn. And in the far corner, I see something stir. The boy in the back has woken up, and I can't help but grin.

After all, it only takes one person to open your eyes to the world.

Janna Graber

3

BEING THERE FOR EACH OTHER

Friends are there when your hopes are
raveled and your nerves are knotted;
talking about nothing in particular,
you can feel the tangles untwist.

Pam Brown

Got Tea?

I've known met Jenny since the day I started taking piano lessons from her mother. Jenny is blonde; I am brunette. All-American Jenny is tall and vivacious. I am petite and quiet. Jenny has a bubbling troupe of siblings; I am an only child. Her favorite flavor is vanilla; I prefer chocolate. Jenny took piano lessons because it was what girls did when they were young, whereas I made music my life.

Our favorite pastime back then was our afternoon tea parties. My first tea set was a Christmas gift the year I was seven. The miniature pieces were decorated with garlands of pink roses and delicate violets. The tea set was accompanied by a charming old trunk filled with all manner of dress-up clothes Mother discovered at the secondhand store. Jenny and I rummaged through the trunk, combining fancy hats, strings of pearls and ecru sweaters with gold buttons until we were pleased with our queenly appearance. We would sit across my child-size table, sipping apple juice and nibbling crackers from the tiny dishes.

Under the Christmas tree every year was a package for the dress-up trunk. Favorite items were kept in the royal collection; others were replaced with new fashion trends. When we were ten, Jenny and I styled each other's hair before foraging through the trunk for high-heeled shoes. With wobbling ankles, we made our way precariously to the kitchen table to pour hot cocoa from Mother's teapot into adult-size mugs, and sample chocolate-chip cookies. And always we talked about our hopes, our dreams and our music.

At thirteen, Jenny and I painted our fingernails with polish and our faces with makeup from the trunk. With a drop of perfume behind each ear, we imagined ourselves as Abigail Adams and Martha Washington discussing the fledgling United States of America, or authors Beatrix Potter and Louisa May Alcott debating book ideas.

For our sixteenth birthdays, Jenny and I pierced our ears. The old trunk held an assortment of brash, dangly earrings we would not wear in public, but which were entirely suitable for tea. Linen napkins across our laps, we savored real tea from Mother's real china tea set, enhanced by slices of banana bread. We made plans to see the world. I would be her bridesmaid, and she promised to be mine.

Eighteen found us on the college rollercoaster. High school graduation flung us at whirlwind speed into the adult world of studies and jobs, cars and insurance, fellows and romance. Jenny's life went one way, mine another. On that vast university campus in fast-paced Southern California, we rarely saw one another.

Except for one special day. We ran into each other on campus and discovered we both had thirty minutes before we needed to be somewhere else. With sudden lightheartedness, we dashed to the nearby café for tea. . . . orange spice for Jenny, raspberry for me. There was so much to talk about. Jenny had met a man with hair as dark as hers was blonde. Work at the art gallery and art studies consumed the rest of her time. I was simultaneously pursuing two doctoral degrees in music and squeezing in a few hours of work. And there was a man in my life.

Those precious free minutes turned into a stolen four hours, and we realized with a start that afternoon classes had long since ended. But sitting on the table between us was a teapot our intuitive waitress had discreetly set there before she left to carry on her life away from the café. The bill read, "On the house."

I married that special man in my life. As promised, Jenny was my bridesmaid. My husband and I set up housekeeping in a vintage house near the college, close to family and friends and all that was dear to me. Jenny and I fit in an occasional cup of tea.

Then everything changed. My husband landed an excellent job with a promising future, great benefits and good salary, all in the field he wanted. He was elated. He said, "The move five hundred miles north would be a terrific adventure."

Adventure? I was devastated. All I knew and was familiar with was here. I needed six more months to complete my studies. I didn't know a soul in the new town so far away. I wasn't one who made friends easily. What would I do there?

Moving so far from loved ones proved extremely difficult. I spent the first days crying as I unpacked boxes in our beautiful new home. Everything felt, and looked, gray.

Then came the first knock on my new door. Standing on the front porch was the mailman with a large parcel. I recognized the return address as Jenny's. Dear, lifelong friend Jenny. Those horrible miles between us melted away, as I tore at the wrapping.

The paper parted to reveal a teapot, decorated with garlands of pink roses and delicate violets. Nestled next to the beautiful china piece was a matching set of teacups and saucers along with a box of raspberry tea. Her note read: "I know you will need a close friend in your new home. You have my permission to find a new close friend. Then you will have two close friends."

Sunday my husband and I visited the nearby church. Renee, an effervescent lady with auburn hair, gave me a hug. "We moved here a year ago, and I know just how lonely you feel."

"Would you come for tea?" I asked.

"I'd be delighted," Renee said with a smile.

Months later, Jenny sent a smaller package, a box of orange spice tea. The enclosed note read, "I'll be there Saturday for tea!" And so Jenny made her first of many visits to our northern home.

When I called Jenny with the news I was expecting our first baby, she sent a package of peppermint tea, to soothe my nauseous tummy.

It's been fifteen years since my husband and I moved North. Renee brought me a beribboned package containing a mug with the picture of an angel and the words, "May your guardian angel keep watch over you when we're apart." Renee and her family were moving out of state.

I sent Renee off with a hug and a package to open on the drive to their new address. The gift bag held a pair of teacups and a note that read: "You will need a close friend in your new home. You have my permission to find one. Then you will have two close friends."

Jenny and I keep in touch mostly by phone. As always, we are startlingly different. Jenny's life takes her to exciting and glamorous places. My world is filled with my three children, carpooling, church and music.

Just last week, Jenny telephoned.

"How wonderful to hear from you," I exclaimed. "But I'm in the middle of giving a piano lesson. Can I call you back?"

"I'm afraid not," she replied with a laugh. "I'm calling

from a layover in a New York airport. I'm putting a package in the mail, some delicious herbal teas from a little shop. I thought of you immediately. It's some of those berry flavors you adore. . . ."

PeggySue Wells

Details

The best time to make friends is before you need them.

Ethel Barrymore

Every minute of the upcoming week was already planned. Just as soon as I returned from dropping off Summer, Emerald, Jesse and their friends at the church campout on a Tillamook beach, it was time to start preparing the house and yard for next weekend's Realtor tour.

Even with help from my eldest and youngest sons, the chore list was daunting. Every growing thing in the garden was indulging in some vegetative height contest. The lawn was a field, the bushes had merged into the surrounding forest and paths had disappeared months earlier. The house wasn't much better. Between school schedules and the weekly five hundred miles to get everyone to various lessons and appointments, the time budgeted for housekeeping shrank from little to nearly none.

Still, this was the last chance to sell the house or face foreclosure, so we intended to vanquish clutter and shrubbery in the next few days and make the place irresistible.

A scant three hours after making the four-hour round-trip, the phone rang. Jesse was sick, and the trip leader was worried because he seemed to be getting hotter very quickly. Hoping it was just tired excitement, I asked to talk to him. "Mom, I really don't feel good," he whispered. "I'm on my way," I told him.

Hollering for my teenage son to pour the pot of espresso I'd made into a Thermos, I pulled on a clean shirt, grabbed keys, purse and Thermos, and headed back.

Jesse was burning up by the time I pulled into the camp at ten that night. Retracing the curvy coastal mountain road, I wondered whether it would be better to stop in some small town to get help. But no, there wouldn't be a hospital, and we'd have to wait for an ambulance or helicopter. The Suburban clung to the road, tires protesting every curve taken too fast. In the middle seat, Jesse slumped sideways, burning and unresponsive.

The emergency room attendant came out to the car, took one look at him and called for a gurney. They sped past admitting and through the self-locking doors of the operating room, leaving me at reception, fumbling for an insurance card.

Within minutes Jesse was hooked up to an IV, antibiotics and hydrating fluids flowing into his veins. The surgeon arrived ten minutes later, shucking her coat without coming to a stop, explaining, as I ran alongside her, "His appendix may have already ruptured. I'll talk to you as soon as I get out." With a *clang,* the doors swung closed behind her, too.

It was 1:15 in the morning. The waiting room outside the operating room was empty.

Finally, the doors opened again, and the surgeon, looking as exhausted as I felt, emerged. Yes, Jesse would be okay, but he would need to stay in the hospital for several days. I would be allowed to stay in his room.

The sun was already starting to rise in the sky when Jesse was wheeled into a room. I sat beside him, watching the light grow outside, waiting for him to wake up.

By seven he was awake and, although subdued, already noticeably improved. The tightness around my heart eased. And when he wondered if he could have ice cream for breakfast, the fear began to release its hold.

Within the hour, the doctor came. Everything looked good. Jesse got a smile from the nurse when he asked for ice cream, although he had to be content with liquids and Jell-O for a few more hours.

As he settled back to sleep, my mind, freed from serious concerns, began to review all that still waited to be done at home. And, who would bring the girls home? Before I could work myself up into a full panic, the door opened and a member of our church arrived, armed with balloons for Jesse and lattes and muffins for us.

When she left, the strain and sleepless hours kicked in, and I curled up on the cot next to Jesse's bed. Just as I drifted off, I silently asked the universe to please take care of everything that needed to be done. "Please, God, take care of the details for me. I'm so tired."

By afternoon, the phone began to ring, and people started calling to check on the patient and offer assistance. Someone notified the trip coordinators in Tillamook, and another parent brought the girls home.

Summer and Emerald arrived at the hospital late that afternoon, just in time for another of my friends to whisk them off, along with their little brother, Larkin, for pizza and ice cream. Friends appeared seemingly out of nowhere to provide rides, run errands and entertain Jesse long enough for me to shower and change.

The handful of days in the hospital went by quickly,

thanks to Jesse's rapid recovery and the constant support of friends and neighbors.

On Friday, Jesse was discharged and we headed home. I realized with horror that I'd forgotten to cancel the next day's open house, and I began making a mental list of everything I'd need to do to catch up on a week's absence.

As we pulled into our driveway, it took a minute to register what was happening. Cars were parked everywhere.

Gardening equipment and buckets were stacked in the carport. From the surrounding garden rose the buzz of weed whackers, brush trimmers and voices, lots of voices.

Momentarily, the din ceased, and friends came over to greet Jesse before returning to their work. In the house, the noise level was lower, but the activity level similar. The children of friends were working with my kids, cleaning the stove, scouring burners, sweeping, vacuuming and organizing cupboards.

After Jesse was settled in on the sofa with juice and a book, I wandered in and out, tired and overwhelmed. Everywhere I turned, a familiar, often grimy, face smiled at me, and grass-covered, dusty arms reached out to hug me.

With a rush of grateful tears, I remembered my sleepy request for help. The universe had responded, placing the details safely into the loving hands of friends.

Lizanne Southgate

Famous Last Words

Oh those dreaded words! But here was my trusted, very best friend calling me and telling me that she was fixing me up on a blind date. *A blind date! Was she out of her mind?* We were juniors in high school and she and I had been the best of friends since first grade. We had grown up together, shared our secrets, shared our parents and had laughed and cried together. *Did she want to end our friendship here and now?* She must have been crazy thinking that she was going to fix me up with her boyfriend's friend. She had never even seen this guy and here she was insisting that we were going to double date and go to Disneyland. And the date was tonight! Was she crazy? I was not going to go out with some strange geek, and I was especially not going to be stuck with that geek at Disneyland for hours and hours. Couldn't we go to a movie instead? At least if we were going to a movie, it would be dark and I wouldn't have to talk to him or look at him.

My friend, Sue, and I had a huge fight. She insisted that I was going on this date, and I insisted that there was no way that I was going. Back and forth we argued. She said that I was just being stubborn—like that mattered. She said that if I didn't go, she couldn't go—like guilt was going to make any difference to me. Who cared? We were at a complete impasse.

I decided to talk to my mother. I knew she would be on my side and back me up. She always did. To my surprise my mother told me that she thought I should go. I couldn't believe my ears. What was my mother doing on Sue's side of the argument? My mother said that I really enjoyed going to Disneyland and, since Sue was going, too, she knew that I would have a good time. Sue and I always had good times together. Then, after the date, we could talk on the phone for hours and hours going over all of the details again and again. After all, it was only for one short evening. My mother said to me, "You're just going to Disneyland—you're not going to marry the guy!"

Famous last words! Not only did I go to Disneyland on that blind date, but four years later I did marry that very same guy! And now, some thirty years later, my blind date, Frank, our three sons and I still tease my mother about her famous last words. And I am still the very best of friends with Sue—who is more like a sister to me than a friend. We still share our secrets and our memories and she still tells me that I am stubborn. Well, we all know which one of us is the stubborn one—and it's not me! She never gives up until she gets her way. And after all of these years she still gives me a hard time about not wanting to go on that blind date. Who knew it would turn out the way that it did? Thanks, Sue.

Barbara LoMonaco

"And guess what? He's practically employed!"

Knowing When

We are so very rich if we know just a few people in a way in which we know no others.

Catherine Bramwell-Booth

After moving to a new state, I looked for ways to meet new people. Then, to my delight, the neighbor living in the duplex behind mine waved in my direction. She shared a friendly smile, offered a warm hello, told me her name was Evelyn, and engaged me in casual conversation. Without pomp and circumstance or either of us being aware of it, we each invited the other into our lives and became friends.

Evelyn's knack for perfect timing never failed to amaze me.

She always knew *when* . . .

In happy times, she knew when to laugh with me and share my joy.

If I was upset, she knew when to bring chocolates and listen while I vented.

During sad moments, she knew when to offer me a tissue so we could cry together.

If I became unsure about something, she knew when to encourage me not to give up.

Her support, whether by phone, visit or note in the mail, always arrived exactly when needed.

One time in particular her knowing *when* saved me. . . .

Our fifth child's delivery date was to be later than expected. Family members, who awaited the SOS call, would be notified quickly so they could come take care of our four children. As time and schedule permitted, my husband, Eddie, would care for our three school-aged boys, but because of his irregular work schedule, he couldn't manage our one-year-old daughter.

My friend Evelyn didn't hesitate. "I'll keep her for as long as you'd like."

It put my mind at rest to know everyone would be taken care of. All I had to do was deliver the baby and return home to the rest of the family as soon as possible.

I went into labor and our plan went into effect.

But, tragically, our baby boy died from complications.

There was nothing anyone could do to ease my pain, heartache and loss.

Four days later, when I returned home from the hospital, I had no idea how to explain to our three sons what had happened. I didn't know how to comfort them in their grief, or me in mine. To my surprise, they offered more comfort than I could give. They stayed at my side and showered me with talk of their school activities. How I appreciated every thoughtful moment. Still, I knew I had to come to grips with my own grief, shock and sorrow.

As the day progressed, to my further horror, my husband became seriously ill and was rushed to the intensive care unit at the local hospital. The threat of a second loss became more than I could bear. *What would I do if Eddie died, too?*

My mother, already en route, arrived that very day and took over the care of the boys.

I didn't call anyone about Eddie, not even Evelyn, who still had our daughter at her house. I could only retreat to my bedroom—to be alone, to think, to brace myself for the worst, to grapple with answers to threatening questions: *How will I ever recover from losing my baby boy? Will I be a single parent of four? How will I make ends meet? Will I have to get a job? Who will take care of the children, a day-care service?* I collapsed on the bed and sobbed, unable to leave my cocoon of grief.

Early the next morning before Eddie's parents arrived, one of the boys came into my bedroom where I remained, wallowing in self-pity and depression. "Mom, Evelyn's here. She's in her car. She said she wasn't sure just when to come in. But she told me she had something she thought would help you feel better."

Somehow I managed to drag myself to the door.

There, parked at the end of the driveway, was Evelyn with my one-year-old daughter who I hadn't seen in over a week. Walking to meet with them, I saw my little girl's face glowing with excitement. She stretched her arms up to me. I started to cry, wondering if she'd thought she'd lost me.

Evelyn opened the door, handed me our baby girl and said, "I think this is the best medicine for you now."

I embraced my daughter, held her close and looked into the eyes of my best friend. "How did you know?"

"The boys called and told me about Eddie. I knew this was when you needed all your family here."

Knowing *when* is an art my friend Evelyn has perfected.

But being this kind of friend is an art perfected only by God.

Helen Colella

Wishing Away

Do you believe that some people are sent into your life to teach you an important lesson? I do! One such special person in my life was Katherine.

At the time I met Katherine, I was an extremely busy single mother, raising three rambunctious children. Life seemed to be a continual merry-go-round of work, home, schedules and activities. My fondest wish involved a deserted island, warm sunny days, an inexhaustible supply of romance novels, and absolute peace and quiet.

I became aware that Katherine had moved into my apartment complex when my seven-year-old daughter, Amber, asked if her new friend could spend the night. "Please? Her name is Joy, and she just moved into number 18 with her mommy."

I stopped making hamburger patties long enough to gaze at my child. Standing next to her was a blue-eyed, blonde-haired, gap-toothed little girl, waiting anxiously for my response. Issuing a resigned sigh, I agreed. "Go get Joy's things. We'll be eating in a half hour." With big grins, the two pint-sized whirlwinds were gone. I continued dinner preparations, wishing that I could be ordering steak in a fine restaurant.

Within minutes the phone rang. Katherine was calling to introduce herself and to confirm the invitation to spend the night. As we chatted, I noted that her words slurred occasionally and wondered if she had a speech impediment. I had little time to ponder Katherine's speech, however. I had children to feed, laundry to do and evening rituals to perform. With a hurried good-bye, I began peeling potatoes as I wished for the late-evening hours when I could retreat to the personal oasis I called "my time."

From that beginning, Joy and Amber were inseparable. I spoke to Katherine on the phone occasionally, but never found the time to meet her. I would glimpse her sitting on a bench by the apartment playground, talking to the children, and wonder how she managed to find the time to spend on such a frivolous activity. Didn't she have a job to go to? Housework to do? Schedules to keep? How I wished I knew the secret of finding time to play. What fun it would be to toss a ball and laugh in the summer sun.

As time passed, I began to notice that Katherine had problems. At times, her speech was difficult to understand. She seemed to stagger and lose her balance. She dropped things. I wondered if she had an alcohol problem and if the girls were safe with her. I decided the time had come to get to know this woman better and invited her to a family dinner.

The evening that Katherine and Joy came to dinner proved to be a pivotal point in my life. I watched her closely as she sat at the table surrounded by children. Her speech was muffled in spots; her movements measured and slow. But I could not detect alcohol on her breath, and she declined the glass of wine I offered.

She seemed happy to focus on the children, listening intently to their stories. She asked them questions and considered their answers seriously. She flittered from topic to topic, keeping pace with their rapid thoughts. She entertained them with amusing stories of her own childhood.

After our meal, the children raced outside to play in what was left of the summer sunshine. Katherine and I followed at a more sedate pace. She walked slowly and carefully while she revealed her past life as a budding executive married to an active, high-profile man. She told me of a lifestyle filled with social activity, vacations, and diverse people and settings. She had lived the life I'd always wished for but never achieved.

We settled on a bench beside the playground and quietly watched the children at their games. I thought of how predictable and unexciting my life was compared to the picture Katherine had painted. With a sigh, I told her how I wished the children were older. Then, I would have more time to do some things for myself.

A small smile crossed her face as Katherine replied, "My only wish is to be able to stay out of a nursing home until Joy is grown. You see, I have multiple sclerosis. It's slowly taking over my body. It's changed my entire life. My husband couldn't deal with being married to an invalid, and I couldn't keep up with my career. Now, all I want is to be able to raise my daughter. I want to share as much of her world as I can for as long as I can. I've learned to treasure every minute of every day with her, because I don't know how many more of those there are left."

Katherine turned to me, and with another smile she continued, "Don't spend your life wishing away what you have. You never know when it will be gone."

Approaching darkness ended our conversation, as we became involved with herding our children to their baths and beds. But later that evening, in that quiet time between wakefulness and sleep, I could hear her words floating through my head and heart, and resolved to appreciate my world instead of wishing for something different.

Time passed quickly, as it always does. Joy and Amber progressed through childhood and adolescence. I spent as much time as I could with them and Katherine. Life was a kaleidoscope of excitement and joy, pain and sorrow. For each stage of development the girls experienced, it seemed Katherine's body paid a price as she slowly deteriorated physically and mentally.

Katherine's wish was granted. She was able to watch Joy receive her high-school diploma, go on to further her education and start a rewarding career.

Some of my many wishes were also granted. The children are now raised and on their own, and I have time to pursue my interests. I have precious grandchildren to keep me focused on the wonders of the world, and friends and family to love and enjoy. And I carry with me the knowledge that I was granted something for which I never wished . . . the rewards of knowing Katherine and learning from her wisdom.

Lana Brookman

A Friend, Indeed

The hearts that never lean, must fall.

Emily Dickinson

It was three in the morning. Rolling over in bed, I reached for the ringing telephone. Instinctively, I knew who it was—who else would be calling at this hour? I had been expecting this call but why did it have to come when I was alone? My husband had just left for the east coast on business eight hours earlier. How would I get in touch with him? I picked up the telephone and heard my mother's voice gently come through the receiver: "Honey, Dad's gone." As if she could read my mind, she quickly assured me that he had not been alone and he had died peacefully.

I assured my mother I would leave for home first thing in the morning but I had to go to work first and reschedule my patients. I hung up the telephone and pulled the covers up. I would let my daughters sleep while I started gathering our things together for the twelve-hour trip home.

I had not turned on the bedside lamp. The house was quiet and dark. I lay in bed thinking about my father's seven-year battle with cancer and what he had taught me. He had said, "When the treatment becomes worse than the disease, it is time to rethink your plan of action." Only one week earlier, I had been at his bedside. I found myself wanting to ensure that those caring for him understood that he was not an old man, but one about to celebrate his fifty-eighth birthday. As a birthday gift, I placed a picture of my father, taken a year earlier, in a frame that had the poem "Footprints" on it. I remember thinking, *This picture looks like a fifty-seven-year-old man.* I looked at the poem. How could I trust God to carry my father if I would not release him to God's care?

The telephone call had been no surprise. I had been holding on to my father and was finally able to entrust him to God, the true healer. Lying in my bed, I silently prayed for any sign to let me know Dad was okay. Seeking reassurance, I drifted off. I was back in my childhood house. My bedroom window was open, allowing the night breeze to blow across my room. I snuggled up under my quilts. I felt warm and safe. I could see my father standing at the foot of my bed. He was checking to see if I was all right before going to bed himself.

As I awoke, I felt a peace flow over me and knew my father was all right. I realized he would always be looking over me. I turned on the lamp and started gathering my things. Dawn came, and I sat down with my daughters. I shared the news of their grandfather's death, trying to ensure that they felt my strength and love enveloping them. I called my friend Carolyne, a fellow visiting nurse, trying to give her a heads-up that I was preparing to go out of town and would be at work to make the appropriate arrangements. Carolyne and I had become good friends as a result of all we did together: working, attending college classes and going to church. Few words were needed for me to inform her of my plan to drive home.

When I reached the office, I realized my coworkers were all aware of my situation and my patients were already reassigned to other nurses. Carolyne proceeded to tell me she had a bag packed and would be driving with me to Washington. Her mother had arranged a return flight for the following day and our supervisor had given her the time off. I was overwhelmed by this generous offer, but I could not ask her to do this. In addition, I knew I would be going straight to my parents' house, which would be filled with family. Where would Carolyne stay? Carolyne told me to call my mother. I made the call so I could graciously say "No thank you" to Carolyne's kind offer. As I spoke to my mother, she breathed a sigh of relief, knowing I would not be alone on the icy roads.

My daughters, Carolyne and I drove straight through to my parents' house. My friend listened as my daughters and I told stories celebrating my father's life. The twelve-hour trip over the mountains went safely and quickly. The healing had begun.

Upon our arrival, my mother's gratitude for our safe arrival was evident. Carolyne was welcomed and thanked profusely. The house was filling up, and Carolyne and I wound up sharing my parents' bed. As we ended our day in prayer and closed our eyes, Carolyne sensed I needed my husband and reassured me that he would be joining me shortly. I smiled to myself knowing this special friend had been sent to carry me when I most needed support.

In the morning, I drove my friend to the airport. She refused my multiple offers to reimburse the cost of her airfare. Instead, she asked me to accept this gift of friendship.

As I drove back to my parents' house, I felt overwhelmed by the goodness of this woman. She had given me a gift that my family and I would never forget.

It has been ten years since my father passed away, and he continues to look over me. Carolyne has become my best friend. We continue to share our love of God, family and nursing. She knows me as few people do, and a special connection and trust exists between us. People often ask if we are sisters. Maybe we are, because there is no doubt in my mind that she is family and my sister in Christ.

Vivia M. Peterson

Hush, Hush, Sweet Charlotte

We have been friends together in sunshine and in shade.

Caroline E. S. Norton

The first time I ever met Charlotte was in the run-down bachelor living room of my serious date, LeRoy Bearman, a cub reporter for the *Albuquerque Journal*. She was nineteen, tall, willowy and dark, from a very well-off Jewish family. She was telling LeRoy's cousin, a much taller, willowy, dark guy, who had just graduated from Harvard Law School, that she didn't use much makeup, and other totally innocuous things which caused a twitch in the right corner of my upper lip. I was twenty-two, a first-generation, short, dark Italian American, in her first year of teaching. A few months later, Charlotte and this guy, Elvin, eloped, taking her parents along as witnesses, departing for a honeymoon out there, probably someplace expensive. Shortly after, LeRoy and I married and honeymooned in a cheap Mexican border town.

The Kanters started life in the American dream home in

the suburbs, and the Bearmans began in a working-class white stucco. Even with the wide contrasts in our lives, Charlotte and I gravitated to each other. She liked my opinionated and resourceful personality, and I was nuts about her open, generous heart and that she was game for anything. The years marched down the pike and we molded our own unique friendship.

"I've got my boy," she pronounced over the phone one day. We were now the mothers of two daughters each.

"You're pregnant?" I quizzed. "When?"

"Last night, and I've got my boy," she answered with certainty. He was born nine months later.

When she told me one day she was hiring garden help, I asked, "Why?"

"They're charging you how much to do one little flower bed?" I hooted. "Listen, get a sitter. I'm coming over. We're going to the store for manure."

All in one day, we shoveled, pickaxed and spread New Mexico's finest, into which we planted a riot of orange and yellow calendulas. When the two of us looked at each other, knee-deep in that honey heap, we fell down laughing and fell in love forever as friends.

"You know, Isabel," she stated, when we could finally garner some control, "there's an old Yiddish proverb that says 'What use is a silver cup if it's full of tears?' Well, what use is my silver cup if it's full of whining and waiting? Charge!"

I taught her things like fastening bolts into a wall to hang plants, mowing grass on a hill, gardening and basic sewing techniques. She taught me about love, that we were a part of a larger community and the finer points of biting my tongue, putting teeth marks in my bottom lip. We both loved cooking, traded methods, recipes and shared all the things young wives do about kids and marriage. She handed me bricks as I laid a brick serpentined wall to divide my patio from the rest of the yard. We gagged back laughter when I cemented a wax paper-wrapped note into the wall, which read: *Isabel made this wall. LeRoy Bearman did not help.*

"I cut the picnic bench in half!" I shrieked into the phone. Fresh out of a carpentry class for dummies, I made the first cut with a circular saw on a board, which should have been the beginning of closet shelves for purses and shoes, "I'm buying you another one night now!" she heralded.

"It's okay," I demurred. "And thank you so much, but I'm keeping this halfer around to remind me about the power of power tools. It could have been my fingers."

After eleven years of marriage, LeRoy, at barely forty-two, suffered a massive heart attack. Charlotte threw everything aside and stayed up all night with me that first night at the hospital. Through those long, dark moments she stood waiting for me outside intensive care surgery when I returned from my allotted visit every half hour. LeRoy had undergone an eight-hour quadruple bypass and wasn't expected to survive the night.

"All I did that awful night was talk about my problems," she confided years after, holding back tears. "I am so sorry. I am so embarrassed. Please forgive me for being so selfish."

"You kept me sane, Charlotte," I choked. "If it hadn't been for you talking about all those normal things—just living life, saying such everyday things—I don't know what I would have done."

LeRoy lived for two more agonizing months and left this earth the first night of Hanukkah. It was Charlotte and Elvin who brought me home to my house brimming with people. She sat quietly on the couch and took the girls into her arms and began to speak softly to them. Completely numb, following her lead, I and other women sat and passed my daughters in turn, giving them comforting words and security, the eternal ageless of a circle of women.

It was in Charlotte and Elvin's home where I remarried a wonderful man three years later.

Two decades passed, and we now met once a month for a quiet supper out. Our talk had gone from diapers to wrinkles. One evening she described a strange pain in her chest, dismissed it and went on to plans for her mother-in-law's ninetieth birthday celebration.

"I have cancer," she told me over the phone soon after. "I didn't want you to hear it from anybody but me. I'm going up to New York for treatment."

The next time I saw my friend, she was paralyzed and bedridden. When I looked at the frail figure with only brittle wisps of hair raked around her thin, bald head I felt the earth come up to meet me. My heart began cracking wide open.

I climbed in the bed right next to her.

"I'm scared," she whispered, laying her head on my shoulder.

"So am I," I responded, swallowing immeasurable grief and terror. An unshed ocean of tears stayed swallowed. "But here we are, together again in a manure pile!"

"Charge!" she croaked.

We laughed so loud.

Throughout the next months, I went almost daily to massage her, to just be with her. We twined our hearts together holding tight, with me having the strength to walk uphill until she would let go. Most evenings her children and close women friends gathered, surrounding her with life, laughter and immeasurable, devoted love. I bought a pile of cards and mailed one a day, writing all our memories down, penning what I couldn't say out loud. My friend, so wide with love, so utterly good and deep with generosity, was going to die at fifty-two. One evening, all the family, including us, gathered in her bedroom to have supper together on TV trays. Beside her sat

Elvin, his head shaved to match hers. The center of all our hearts, she was cuddled up and smiling in the large bed, head wrapped in a gay, flowered turban.

It was the last time I saw her.

When Charlotte had rallied, I took a few days to go to Colorado with friends. Elvin called a half hour after I'd arrived to say it was bad. Somehow, I made it aboard an old smoke-belching yellow bus that coughed around mountain curves all the way to the Denver airport. I begged a seat on a two-engine puddle-hopper that literally rocked and rolled over snow-covered mountaintops, landing at the Albuquerque airport, I was completely airsick and shaken.

"She's gone, Mamma," Erica, my eldest daughter, choked out, rushing me through baggage. "She asked that you sing for her."

Crouched down on the backseat, I threw off hiking boots and jeans and wriggled into a dress she'd brought.

The synagogue was filled to overflowing.

I can't do this, I said to myself.

"You did it—we did it that night for LeRoy," came her voice. "We'll get through this one together, too."

Climbing the steps to the bema, a burst of sunlight filled the room. It became just Charlotte and me. I saw us holding our babies, washing towers of dishes, cooking for hordes of people, potty training puppies and kids, and sitting in that manure pile. "Sunshine on My Shoulders" just came out, followed by some Jewish songs she'd taught me; then I just stood, looked up at that skylight and began.

"Hush, hush, sweet Charlotte. Charlotte, don't you cry. Hush, hush, sweet Charlotte. I'll love you till I die."

Many years have passed. There isn't a day that goes by that I don't take the path to her house in my heart. There isn't a day that I don't miss her, because you can walk waist-deep in platitudes, but they, time, and all the words and living in the world can't replace the presence—the normal closeness, the company of someone beloved. Three years ago, at a little place we own up north, I hauled a ton of manure, dug a big hole and put in the most beautiful big Rocky Mountain blue spruce I could move. For three summers now, I often sit, head propped on Charlotte's feathery branches and gaze at the little stream in front of our cabin.

"Hush, hush, sweet Charlotte," I sing. "I'll love you till I die . . . and after, too."

"Hush, hush, sweet Isabel," she answers. "Me, too. I'll see you soon."

Isabel Bearman Bucher

The Icing on the Cake

It takes a lot of understanding, time and trust to gain a close friendship with someone. As I approach a time of my life of complete uncertainty, my friends are my most precious asset.

Erynn Miller

Sharyn found life on the sidelines to be disconcerting.

Oh, sure, acquaintances stopped in, church members phoned regularly, and her sons kept in contact and ran errands. But she missed prowling the mall with girlfriends, participating in church meetings, even purchasing her own groceries. She missed running her own errands and puttering in the yard. She missed going. She missed doing.

And now, it seemed, she would miss her son's December wedding.

Sharyn had dealt with illness her entire life. As a newborn, she suffered from rickets, and her health only proceeded to worsen. Allergies, asthma and other ailments hounded her until now, at fifty-five, her problems read like the index to a medical text:

Arthritis
Bedsores
Collagen disease
Degenerative osteoporosis

Sharyn needed heart and lung transplants, but wasn't a candidate for either. Instead, committed to an elaborate schedule of pharmaceuticals, tethered to an oxygen tank and confined to a wheelchair, Sharyn teased that she preferred spending her time traveling. Traveling between her two homes: the house and the hospital. Actually, going anywhere else was out of the question, especially to her son's out-of-state wedding ceremony.

Because no plane, train or car could accommodate Sharyn's delicate health needs, she resigned herself to staying home while the rest of the family attended the wedding . . . without her. They left her with tender promises to remember all the details, to take lots and lots of pictures, and to save her some wedding cake.

During her husband's absence, caregivers saw to her meals and personal needs, but Sharyn couldn't shake her blues and feelings of isolation. It wasn't easy finding herself apart from her family at Christmas and missing the festivities of her son's wedding. The hurt followed her as surely as the oxygen tube trailing her wheelchair.

But she hadn't counted on Vickie.

Vickie arrived with Big Plans: an old-fashioned girl-friends' slumber party. She surprised Sharyn by bringing along her own holiday guest, their mutual friend Carol. She supplied chocolates to nibble, popcorn to munch, sodas to drink . . . and a lively video to watch from bed later that night. The three gabbed and giggled away the hours, pausing only to click on the lamps when evening dimmed the room.

And they talked about everything under the sun—everything, that is, except the wedding Sharyn was missing.

Instead, the two women bundled their fragile friend against the bitter Kansas wind and, with meticulous timing and coordination, managed to pack Sharyn—wheelchair, oxygen tank and all—into Vickie's van. Chirping like excited elves, the three headed out for their version of a night on the town: a tour of attractive Christmas displays scattered around the small-town neighborhoods. They *oohed* over animated vignettes. They *aahed* at each crèche. They pointed out ribbon-wrapped wreaths, a window lit in peaceful blue and a lawn festooned in red candy canes. But Vickie saved the best for last.

"Now, Sharyn, close your eyes while I turn the corner to this house." She maneuvered the car down the gravel road and stopped. "Okay, you can look."

Sharyn opened her eyes and gasped.

Sparkling, twinkling and winking, thousands of tiny white lights outlined the winding drive like intricate frosting on a cake. A fantasy of winter white, they swagged the rows of arbors that canopied its entire length, like a powdering of a delicate angel dust.

The van inched its way under, through and along the enchanting path; the women barely breathed, wide-eyed and wordless.

"Oh, look!" Sharyn whispered. "It's beautiful enough for a bride." Her voice caught. "Why, it's like a . . . a bridal arch!"

A sacred silence softened the air as all three pondered the thought.

"You know, Vickie," Sharyn murmured into the hush, "others will bring home a piece of cake. But only a friend like *you* would bring me a piece of the wedding."

Carol McAdoo Rehme

I'm Going to Buy a Paper Doll . . .

I have learned that to have a good friend is the purest of all God's gifts, for it is a love that has no exchange of payment.

Frances Farmer

Most Sunday afternoons after church, my best friend, Pat, and I sat huddled close together at the dining room table, sharing crayons, paper and scissors, and making clothes for the latest paper doll figures that appeared in the funnies section of the paper that day.

We would patiently draw around the forms of the dolls, always remembering to include the essential tabs at all the right places so the clothes would stay on, and then begin designing the most elegant and beautiful, or outrageous, costumes eight-year-olds could imagine.

After we were satisfied with our pencil work, we colored them, cut them out and added the latest creations to the decorated shoe boxes that we pretended were steamer trunks.

This entire adventure with paper dolls, as I remember,

consisted not so much of actually playing with them, but in seeing which of us could make the prettiest clothes. Pat usually won the competition. Even at an early age she had a certain flair, which makes me sad that she didn't pursue a career in fashion design.

Our fascination with paper dolls lasted for several years, until Sunday afternoon activities began to center more and more around our own clothes, experiments with makeup and boys. After high school, Pat married a local boy and started a family, then became a widow a few years later when her husband died suddenly and unexpectedly.

Following high school, I went away to college, married and lived in the East for a few years. During the time I was away from Texas, Pat left our hometown and moved to be near her dad, both as an escape from her memories and for help in raising three young children. Our contact over the ensuing thirty-plus years was limited to birthday and Christmas cards, occasional telephone calls, and even less occasional visits. Despite this, we remained best friends.

I had not thought about our paper doll days in a long, long time. That is, until about a month ago, when I learned my best friend, Pat, was terminally ill with cancer in both kidneys.

Three weeks ago, I went to see her. As I drove, I rehearsed over and over in my mind what I would do and say. Even that didn't prepare me enough. I found Pat, who had always been doll-sized compared to my generous frame, swollen to twice her normal size, having difficulty breathing and unable to do basic things like bathing or preparing a meal for herself.

After hugs of greeting, we sat down at her kitchen table and over coffee, talked about how spring was early this year, what our children and grandchildren were doing, and how long it had been since our last visit. Our conversation then shifted to more serious matters: the pain she was having, the terrible side effects of the medication she was taking and how she was managing financially, since she could no longer work.

She looked puzzled when I finally opened the shopping bag I'd brought and took out a shoe box, some crayons, lined paper and a pair of snub-nosed scissors. Her puzzled look vanished when I handed her the Barbie paper doll book. Leafing through it, we commented on how the books still didn't have enough pages of clothes. Then, just like so many years before, we huddled close together and began designing the most elegant and beautiful, or outrageous, clothes we fifty-year-olds could imagine. Afterward, we held hands and cried.

I am glad I went to see her, although it was one of the hardest things I've ever done. For a brief time, we laughed and talked just like old times, and I noticed as I hugged her good-bye, her eyes seemed brighter than when I'd arrived.

Pat died just two days after my visit, but I won't forget her. Or my mother's words of long ago: "Remember, honey, God only gives us one best friend in a lifetime."

Carol J. Rhodes

Getting It Right

The only thing to do is to hug one's friends tight and to do one's job.

Edith Wharton

On the April morning I found out about Lucy's mother, it rained. A light, cooling sprinkle of tears that grayed the Texas sky. I didn't know what kind of cancer Mrs. Hastings had until later, but I knew her condition was serious— very serious.

Now don't get me wrong. I love Mr. and Mrs. Hastings almost as much as I love my own parents, and Lucy is my best friend. But I didn't want to go to school that day. And I sure didn't want to see Lucy.

What could I possibly say to her? What do people say to their friends at such a time? I was afraid to send Mrs. Hastings so much as a get-well card because I wasn't sure she was going to get well. I tried every trick I knew to get out of going to school. But Mom insisted.

"You have a history test this morning, Kristin," she said, looking at me as if she'd crawled into my mind and knew

I was just making excuses. "Had you forgotten?"

"No, Mother, I hadn't forgotten."

She smiled. "Be sure to stay close to Lucy, especially today, because that poor girl is going to need your strength."

Strength? What was Mother talking about? I had no strength. I didn't even know what to say to my best friend.

I hid out in the choir room between classes in hopes of avoiding Lucy, but she was never out of my thoughts. I kept trying to come up with something appropriate to say to her because I really wanted to get it right. I even wrote out a dialogue between the two of us, but in the end, I tore it up because it simply didn't sound like me.

Lucy and I had last-period English in Mrs. Green's room. Though I'd eluded her all day, I was going to have to face her last period, and I still didn't have a plan. However, I worried needlessly because Lucy never showed up for class.

When English class was over, Mrs. Green said, "Kristin, I know Lucy Hastings is your best friend, and I would like to know how she is handling her mother's illness."

"I don't know how she's handling anything," I said, "because I haven't seen or heard from Lucy since yesterday."

"Well, you'll be seeing her shortly because Lucy is coming here in a few minutes to get her lesson assignments."

"Lucy is coming here?"

Mrs. Green nodded. My heart tightened into a hard knot and I trembled inwardly. I still didn't know what to say to Lucy, and time was running out.

"Excuse me, Mrs. Green," I finally said, "but I have to— to go now." I bolted from the classroom.

I raced down the hall and out the front door of school practically in one breath, joining the students who were headed for the campus parking lot.

It had stopped raining, and the air smelled clean and fresh. A rainbow cut across a sky still darkened by thunderclouds, and the wind tossed my hair in all directions until I pulled up the hood of my yellow raincoat.

In the distance I saw someone coming toward me. I knew it was Lucy even though I couldn't see her face. She had her head down, and she was wearing a yellow raincoat exactly like mine. She'd pulled her hood up, too; maybe she hadn't seen me. Maybe if I ran back inside and hid in the choir room again, she wouldn't find me.

Then I noticed how Lucy's shoulders shook with every step she took. And I knew she must be crying because I was. The rain came down again. Raindrops mingled with my tears. Lucy's heart was breaking, and I wasn't doing a thing to help her.

As I drew nearer to her, my throat tightened, making it impossible to speak, even if I'd known what to say. A deep ache filled my heart. I prayed for strength, the strength my mother claimed I already had, and I forced myself to move forward, arms outstretched.

"Oh, Kristin," Lucy cried. "I was hoping it was you."

We hugged then, but I still couldn't utter a sound.

Looking back, I learned something that day that I might never have grasped in any other way. You see, I'd been focusing on me: *What should I do? How should I act? What will I say to Lucy?*

But when we finally came face-to-face, I forgot me and centered on Lucy and her needs. When I did that, I was able to share Lucy's grief—let her know that she was special and that I really cared.

Since then, Lucy has told everyone she sees that I have the gift of saying just the right words at just the right time. I still don't think she realizes that on the day we hugged in the April rain, I never said a word.

Molly Noble Bull

READER/CUSTOMER CARE SURVEY

CDC

We care about your opinions. Please take a moment to fill out this Reader Survey card and mail it back to us.
As a special **"thank you"** we'll send you exciting news about interesting books and a valuable **Gift Certificate.**

Please PRINT using ALL CAPS

First Name			MI.	Last Name	

Address

City | ST | Zip

Phone # ( ) — Fax # ( ) —

Email

(1) Gender:
____ Female ____ Male

(2) Age:
____ 12 or under ____ 40-59
____ 13-19 ____ 60+
____ 20-39

(3) Marital Status
____ Married
____ Single
____ Divorced/Widowed

(4) Did you receive this book as a gift?
____ Yes ____ No

(5) How many Chicken Soup books have you bought or read?
____ 1 ____ 2-4 ____ 5+

(6) How did you find out about this book?
Please fill in ONE.
1) ____ Recommendation
2) ____ Store Display
3) ____ Bestseller List
4) ____ Online
5) ____ Advertisement
6) ____ Catalog/Mailing
7) ____ Interview/Review (TV, Radio, Print)

(7) Where do you usually buy books?
Please fill in your top TWO choices.
1) ____ Bookstore
2) ____ Religious Bookstore
3) ____ Online
4) ____ Book Club/Mail Order
5) ____ Price Club (Costco, Sam's Club, etc.)
6) ____ Retail Store (Target, Wal-Mart, etc.)

(9) What subjects do you enjoy reading about most? Rank only *FIVE*. Use 1 for your favorite, 2 for second favorite, etc.

	1	2	3	4	5
1) Parenting/Family	○	○	○	○	○
2) Relationships	○	○	○	○	○
3) Recovery/Addictions	○	○	○	○	○
4) Health/Nutrition	○	○	○	○	○
5) Christianity	○	○	○	○	○
6) Spirituality/Inspiration	○	○	○	○	○
7) Business Self-Help	○	○	○	○	○
8) Teen Issues	○	○	○	○	○
9) Sports	○	○	○	○	○

(14) What attracts you most to a book?
(Please rank 1-4 in order of preference.)

	1	2	3	4
14) Title	○	○	○	○
15) Cover Design	○	○	○	○
16) Author	○	○	○	○
17) Content	○	○	○	○

TAPE IN MIDDLE; DO NOT STAPLE

BUSINESS REPLY MAIL

FIRST-CLASS MAIL PERMIT NO 45 DEERFIELD BEACH, FL

POSTAGE WILL BE PAID BY ADDRESSEE

CHICKEN SOUP FOR THE GIRLFRIEND'S SOUL
HEALTH COMMUNICATIONS, INC.
3201 SW 15TH STREET
DEERFIELD BEACH FL 33442-9875

FOLD HERE

Do you have your own Chicken Soup story that you would like to send us? Please submit separately to: Chicken Soup for the Soul, P.O. Box 30880, Santa Barbara, CA 93130

Comments:

4

SPECIAL
MOMENTS

When we express our gratitude for others, important things happen to them and us. We are renewed in friendship and love. We are restored emotionally and spiritually. And we are inspired to learn how much we really mean to each other.

Karen O'Connor

The Starter Jar

The language of friendship is not in words, but meanings.

Henry David Thoreau

Our family get-togethers meant abundant food spread out on the dining room table and kitchen counters. Aunts, uncles and cousins balanced plates on laps and tried to catch up on news since the last time. As always, the meal lasted until no one could take another bite.

Today was no exception, making it hard to leave.

"We've got to go," my husband, Allen, said to me and our five-year-old daughter, Meredith. We climbed in the Jeep as the sun that had peeked out of the clouds began to slide behind the tall Georgia pines. Allen started backing out of the drive.

"Wait!" my thirty-eight-year-old cousin, Doug, yelled.

I rolled the window down as he sauntered to the car, never one to be in a hurry.

"You forgot your sourdough bread," he said in his slow Southern drawl. "And here is your starter jar so you can make it." He pushed through the window a glass jar containing what looked like a white, gooey blob.

I stared at the jar tucked into a large Baggie filled with ice and wondered how I would get the strange substance home without creating a mess. Somehow, I balanced the jar between Meredith's toys and a suitcase, and hoped for the best during the upcoming four-hour drive.

"Here's the recipe to make it," Doug added. "It will last indefinitely if you keep feeding it with equal amounts of flour and water, and a tiny bit of sugar." He smiled. "Put it in the refrigerator when you get home, but don't forget it. Like friendships, you have to tend it."

After one more hug, Doug said, "Bake some and invite your friends over."

"Me?" I asked. "You know I'm too busy to bake."

"Make time," he shot back. "It's important to spend time with your friends, to have fun. I take loaves to the ladies who live at the lake all the time. They love it." He grinned.

As we drove home, I remembered how Mom had said that Doug made it a point to get to know his neighbors, mostly retirees. "They're always having dinner parties," she had said.

Now, six months later, I peered into the refrigerator and moved food around to look for the ketchup for Meredith's hamburger. I stopped cold. My knees buckled, and I could only stare at the jar in the back next to the light. The ache behind my eyes spread down to my throat. Tears began to flow as I wrapped my fingers around the jar and pulled it out. I held it close to my chest for what seemed like an eternity.

Finally, I put Doug's starter jar on the counter and rummaged through the drawer by the refrigerator, determined to find the recipe he had given me.

Once I found it, I sat on the floor and stared at his handwriting. I ran my fingers over the words and read the steps that Doug had taken to make the starter mixture. *Wow. He went to a lot of trouble,* I thought.

I held the mixture Doug had prepared, thinking of how he had let it stand in a warm place for seventy-two hours. How he had stirred it two or three times, daily. Even after he placed the fermented mixture in the refrigerator, he had had to stir it once a day. *And he had done this again and again for others?*

At his funeral, it was evident that he had done just that. Even on the Fourth of July, people from all walks of life came to mourn his tragic death. All were shocked over the early morning head-on collision and fiery crash of the young D.O.T. captain returning home from his shift, a mere week before the start of the Olympic Games in Atlanta, where his department was assigned to security. To the bereaved who stared at the closed casket, it was bread bitter to the taste unless your faith rested firmly in the Lord.

But now as I sat on the floor, emotionally spent, I couldn't dwell on the grief. For the first time since his death, I wanted to remember the Doug who put so much effort into making time for fellowship and hospitality, for friends getting together.

He had been right. *You can't let a hectic life keep you from enjoying life—and your friends.* Fortunately, he hadn't.

Suddenly, it was important that I make Doug's bread. I gathered the dry active yeast, all-purpose flour, sugar, salt and warm water—all readily available ingredients to make bread. *Essential food for the body and good to the taste just like friendship,* I could almost hear Doug saying.

Several days later, the delicious scent of baking bread wafted through the house. I picked up the phone and called my neighbor.

"Becky," I said, "don't faint, but I've been baking." I paused and looked over at the starter jar I had made for her. "I know that I've been neglecting my friends," I confessed, "so how about coming over for some sourdough bread? We need to catch up."

Debra Ayers Brown

Saying Good-Bye

Mourning is not forgetting . . . It is an undoing.
Every minute tie has to be untied and something
permanent and valuable recovered and assimilated
from the dust.

Margery Allingham

The weather put on one of its grandest shows on the day of my friend Teri's funeral service. A radiant sun shone down on us as we entered the church, and a gentle breeze swirled the women's skirts. It was as if Mother Nature herself insisted that Teri leave us in proper style.

"The sorrow is ours," her son Jeff said in his moving eulogy.

And it was.

Teri wasn't famous. Her photo never once appeared in any magazine, and her name wasn't one of the "regulars" in any society column.

But if you lived in our little South Jersey town for any length of time, you knew Teri. She was the kind of woman who reached out to newcomers, as well as to the lonely and the lost. And she swept them all up into her incredible embrace.

If you lived on the east side of town, you probably recognized the house on the quiet corner, the one with the tire swing and the tiny lady out on the lawn, typically surrounded by hordes of children.

Teri had six of her own. Plus, eight grandchildren. In this day and age, such families are all but extinct. So the kids and grandkids were semi-celebrities, if only because there were so many of them. Besides that, they were terrific: diverse, interesting, funny, fun.

For more than two decades, my husband and I lived around the corner from Teri and her gang. It was Teri who reached out to us when we were "the new kids on the block," and who saw to it that we got to know the other people in the neighborhood.

Connection was Teri's gift. In a got-to-have-a-gimmick world, she had none. In a culture that measures who you are by what you do, Teri had no snappy résumé. Not unless you counted her unique brand of faith, love and charity.

She was a bright, thoughtful, interested and interesting woman, whose best work was home and family. She was wise without ever reminding you that she was. And if you think that's not much, then you probably wouldn't have had much time for Therese Marie, the name she was given at birth but that nobody ever used.

Our Teri needed no spotlight in order to shine.

I never had a conversation with my friend and neighbor that didn't leave me with some new idea rattling around in my head. I never left one of her parties without thinking, *Now why can't all parties be like that?*

Forget fancy food. Forget pretension. At this house, what you got was a zany kind of pleasure that was easier to feel than to explain. Teri was the Pied Piper of joyous abandon, a child disguised as an adult. Little ones adored her. And big ones did, too.

Every pew was filled at the memorial service for my dear friend. Long after the service was over, we lingered outside the church where we had heard a son eulogize his mother, reminding us of how she made every moment important. Our town's main street had become a moving sea of Teri fans, each of us with our own Teri story.

So many of us felt bereft. And terribly cheated. Death had ambushed Teri in a matter of days, not weeks or months. And few of us had time for a proper good-bye.

Many of us still clutched the little memorial card distributed at the church. On the card was printed a prayer of Saint Francis of Assisi, which read, in part, "Where there is hatred, let me show love. Where there is sadness, joy." So quintessentially Teri, those notions.

It seemed hard to part from our neighbors and friends on that sparkling morning. It seemed odd that in the distance, traffic moved, people shopped and the world went about its business. But outside the church, we couldn't seem to mobilize.

Some of us needed to be near her husband, to surround this man who had been married to Teri for fifty-one years. We could only imagine the anguish he was facing.

Some needed to be near Teri's six children who had just said the hardest good-bye.

On the way home from the memorial service, riding in stunned silence, we passed Teri's house. There were no kids outside; no bicycles heaped against the hedges.

And for the first time in ages, the tire swing was empty.

Sally Friedman

The Gift of Baby Drowsy

My best friend is the one who brings out the best in me.

Henry Ford

Lauri and I have been friends since we were four years old. "I was *four and a half*," I can hear her correcting me, never one to let me forget that she was six months older. When we learned we were related (her grandmother and my great-grandmother were sisters), it only served to solidify our bond as "cousins forever."

Our relationship, however, got off to a somewhat rocky start over an incident involving a permanent marker and my beloved Baby Drowsy doll. I cried for days after Lauri's attempt to do a "makeover" on Drowsy. My older sister tried removing the ink with various household solvents, which, unfortunately, ended up removing some of Drowsy's trademark painted, sleepy eyes, leaving her with somewhat of a permanent wink. But somehow, our friendship managed to survive that ordeal and much, much more.

Of the two of us, Lauri was the rebel—the friend who could turn any playdate into an adventure (or a stint on house arrest if we played our cards right). Lauri was the first girl in our class to come to school wearing makeup. She thought the pale green eye shadow she borrowed from her sister perfectly matched with the green plaid of our hideous school uniforms. Unfortunately, Sister Maria, the principal at our Catholic grade school, didn't agree. In hindsight (and probably because she now has daughters of her own), Lauri will concede that third grade might have been a little early to start wearing makeup.

I give Lauri the credit for all the times we tested the limits and earned the consequences that ensued. Like the time she got us kicked out of Brownies. Okay, we weren't literally *kicked out*, but when the leader asked our moms not to send us back the following year, we took that as a strong hint. I really don't understand why. Maybe it had something to do with the fact that Lauri fell into the creek when we were on litter pickup, and I laughed till I nearly wet my pants. Or perhaps it was the time when we visited that dairy farm. As I recall, it was Lauri who touched off a chain of events that eventually left one Brownie skidding knees first into a pile of cow manure. Looking back, I suppose my belly laughs over that event could have been construed as "encouraging her misbehavior," but I challenge anyone to be in Lauri's presence and not end up roaring with laughter—she was just plain fun to be around. I could tell instantly when she would get that sparkle in her eyes and a smile would start to creep across her face that she had some wonderfully mischievous idea that would likely land us in trouble, but the adventure would certainly be worth any punishment that followed.

All too soon though, our carefree, mischievous childhood days faded away, as the road to adulthood loomed ahead. Through all the obstacles and challenging times I have faced, Lauri has been the one loyal fixture in my life. Despite going to different high schools, we were always there for each other through every imaginable teenage tragedy. From bad perms to broken hearts, I always knew Lauri was just a phone call away—always there to listen and to give advice when sought, but never to judge. We celebrated every triumph and consoled every heartbreak with a scoop of praline pecan ice cream from Baskin-Robbins or a slice of mushroom pizza.

When life dealt me heartache, Lauri was there. The day I buried my baby girl, three weeks after her premature birth, Lauri held my hand and wiped my tears, feeling the loss as much as I did.

Last year, when her father passed away after a long bout with cancer, even though I now lived nine hundred miles away, I knew I had to be there for Lauri. After all, I think I spent more time at her house growing up than I did at my own. Her parents were like surrogate parents to me. So I went to the funeral with the intention of being strong and supportive for my friend, like she was for me in my time of sorrow, but it was Lauri who put her arm around me as I sobbed over her father's casket, giving me a little more of her endless strength. But that's my friend, always putting others first.

It was during this trip back home that Lauri gave me a very special present. "For some reason, when I saw this, I thought of you," she laughed. I could almost see that sparkle of youth coming back into her eyes, as that smile I remembered so well crept across her face when she handed me the package. "I've been meaning to mail it to you, but . . ." her words trailed off as I opened the box. I could not believe my eyes. Lying inside was a brand-new Baby Drowsy doll. I gazed lovingly at her pink and white polka-dotted outfit, my hand gently caressing that silky, blonde hair, and instantly I was swept back to 1975.

"Where . . . where, did you ever . . . ?" I stammered quietly, my now teary eyes still fixated on the cherub-faced doll.

"Mattel is marketing them as *retro dolls*. Doesn't *that* make you feel old?" she quipped, instantly turning my tears to laughter.

"Yes, that does make me feel old," I retorted, wiping my cheek. "But I can only imagine how *you* must feel, being *six months* older than me!" I added, finally seizing the opportunity to exploit being younger after all these years. We both shared a good laugh during a difficult time, but like I said, that's how it is with my best friend—she always makes you laugh.

Life would not be complete without someone like Lauri there to live it with you. That someone who, when you pick up the phone and call her, whether it's been a week or six months, you pick up right where you left off—just as if you had spoken an hour before. Her friendship has truly been a gift to me—much more precious than the Baby Drowsy doll she gave me—and one I'll always treasure.

Jodi L. Severson

copyright kathy shaskan 2003

"I'm afraid I can't be friends with you anymore,
Violet. You have too much baggage."

Sunshine

It is a sweet thing, friendship, a dear balm, a happy and auspicious bird of calm.

Shelbey Shelley

The silence was almost unbearably uncomfortable. I was too nervous to speak, and I think everyone else was, too. The car ride seemed endless. Once in a while, we would look at each other and force a smile, but our smiles were more nervous than warm.

I don't know what she was thinking about, but I know that memories flooded my mind. I was remembering my first day of school, when I felt like there was a spotlight shining on me and someone had written "new" on my forehead. She simply looked at me, took my hand and said, "Come on. I'll help you find your homeroom."

Then there was the time I missed the winning foul shot in a sixth-grade basketball game. The other team was up by one point, and I got fouled just as the buzzer went off. I was allowed one-and-one foul shots, but I missed the first one and the other team won the game. I was angry at myself and apologetic to my team. I felt as though I had let the whole world down. I sat on the bleachers with my head in my hands. Suddenly, I felt her hand rest on my shoulder and a flood of warmth and understanding ran through me. When I looked up, she saw how crushed I was, and tears came to her eyes. She hugged me and told me the story of when she knocked herself out with her own hockey stick during a game. Laughter quickly overcame my tears.

She was also right there when my first boyfriend broke up with me. As I hung up the phone, I could feel tears making my throat close. I felt as though someone had taken my heart away from me in a matter of minutes. She hugged me, and I clung to her as though she were the only thing I had left in the world. Somehow I knew everything would be all right.

As I came back from my daydreams, I realized that our road trip was almost at its end. Only one hour left. She started twirling her hair like she does when she gets nervous. I saw a single tear roll down her cheek. It seemed to take the rest of the car ride for it to reach her chin.

When we drove onto the enormous campus, the rainstorm that had mysteriously appeared was subsiding. We found our way to her assigned dorm, unpacked her things and were standing at the car about to say our good-byes; I couldn't do it. I couldn't say good-bye. We stared at each other, tears streaming down our faces. One long hug and a kiss on the cheek were our farewell. I climbed into the car and strapped on my seat belt.

She sat down in the grass and watched us pull out of the driveway. I stared through the rearview mirror at my best friend whom I was leaving behind at college. I stared until the car turned the corner and buildings blocked my view of my sister who was also my best friend. I looked up into the sky, and through the leftover clouds I saw one single bright ray of sunshine. It was going to be okay.

Sarah Wood

A Forever Friend

Friends may move away—so far that you may never meet again. And yet they are a part of you forever.

Pam Brown

I ended up sitting next to Julie by chance at a motivational seminar. We had ample opportunity to tell stories about ourselves and found that we shared a common interest: passion for the spiritual and "unseen" parts of life. I told her I was studying dreamwork. This interest was to become the glue that bound our lives together. At the end of the day, we exchanged business cards and promised to meet again soon.

When we got together for lunch, Julie casually mentioned that she'd been having random and disturbing pains in her lower legs. The next few months proved to be an emotional and pivotal time in Julie's life. She was becoming increasingly immobilized from the pain and from muscle spasms. Numerous physicians, including neurologists, attempted to diagnose the growing lack of control of her extremities. After endless agonizing tests, Julie had no conclusive answers. She began doing research of her own.

I had never really understood what Lou Gehrig's disease (amyotrophic lateral sclerosis or ALS) was until Julie's research pointed to it as the insidious illness causing her affliction. She educated me about the symptoms, treatments, side effects and, worst of all, prognosis. Unfortunately, the suspicions of her research were confirmed.

Five years after I met Julie, she knew her time was short. We had many conversations concerning her beliefs about death and dying, how she did not want to be a burden and wanted to pass from this existence with dignity. Julie's conversations with God increased in frequency. Near the end, she heard a voice tell her it was time for her to move from her home into a hospice care facility.

By that time, Julie talked often about wanting to leave this Earth, saying that she was ready to go. This was a difficult yet special time for me, as I learned to honor the present moment when visiting her. Time was running out for us. My dear friend was in the active stages of dying. During our last visit together, we made a pact. She said she would contact me, if at all possible, after her death. Due to an out-of-town commitment that could not be postponed, I was not present at Julie's memorial service. A month later, my husband and I went to our beach cabin for the weekend. There, I was able to heal and reflect on this amazingly strong and courageous woman who had taught me so much about the miracle of the human spirit.

On our second night there, I had a very real and intense dream of Julie actually standing in our bedroom. She was radiant, vibrant and smiling just as she had been when I first met her. She opened her arms to me and hugged me hard, then held me at arm's length so that I could see her eyes and her joy. Julie said clearly, "We do not die!" This was more than a dream—I knew I had experienced something very real. It made sense for Julie to contact me this way. She knew my life's work was based on art and dreams. I shook my husband awake and told him that Julie had visited me, what she said and how wonderful she looked.

On the way home, I could not stop thinking about the feeling and image of Julie. I began to cry and thought to myself: *Julie, your strength and spirit and amazing courage touched many lives and hearts. I, for one, will never be the same for having known you.*

Before reaching home, we stopped by our offices to pick up the weekend mail. I found that I had been sent a program from Julie's memorial service. When I opened the envelope, there was Julie's radiant, smiling face on the cover of the leaflet. It was the exact image of her I had seen in my dream! A Native American poem that Julie had selected before her death was printed on the inside page. It began with the words: "Do not sit at my grave and weep, for I am not there. The last line read: "Do not stand at my grave and cry, for we do not die."

Marlene King

A Perfect Pot of Tea

There are high spots in all of our lives and most of them have come about through encouragement from someone else. I don't care how great, how famous or successful a man or woman may be, each hungers for applause.

George M. Adams

An impatient crowd of nearly two hundred die-hard bargain hunters shoved their way into the huge living room of the old Withers homestead. The sweltering ninety-degree temperature didn't deter a single one, all in pursuit of the estate-sale find of the summer.

The lady conducting the sale, a longtime acquaintance, nodded as we watched the early-morning scavengers. "How's this for bedlam?" she chuckled.

I smiled in agreement. "I shouldn't even be here. I have to be at the airport in less than an hour," I admitted to her. "But when I was a teenager, I sold cosmetics in this neighborhood. And Hillary Withers was my favorite customer."

"Then run and check out the attic," she suggested.

"There are plenty of old cosmetics up there."

Quickly, I squeezed through the ever-growing throng and climbed the stairs to the third floor. The attic was deserted except for a petite, elderly woman presiding over several tables loaded with yellowed bags of all sizes.

"What brings you all the way up here?" she asked, as she popped the stopper out of a perfume bottle. "There's nothing up here except old Avon, Tupperware and Fuller Brush products."

I drew in a long, cautious breath. The unmistakable fragrance of "Here's My Heart" perfume transported me back nearly twenty years.

"Why, this is my own handwriting!" I exclaimed, as my eyes fell upon an invoice stapled to one of the bags. The untouched sack held more than a hundred dollars' worth of creams and colognes—my very first sale to Mrs. Withers.

On that long-ago June day, I'd canvassed the wide, tree-lined avenue for nearly four hours, but not one lady of the house had invited me indoors. Instead, several had slammed their doors in my face. As I rang the bell at the last house, I braced myself for the now-familiar rejection.

"Hello, ma'am. I'm your new Avon representative," I stammered, when the carved-oak door swung open. "I have some great products I'd like to show you." When my eyes finally found the courage to face the lady in the doorway, I realized it was Mrs. Withers, the bubbly, matronly soprano in our church choir. I'd admired her lovely dresses and hats, dreaming that someday I'd wear stylish clothes, too.

Just two months before, when I'd traveled to a distant city to have brain surgery, Mrs. Withers had showered me with the most beautiful cards. Once she'd even tucked in a Scripture verse: "I can do all things through Christ which strengtheneth me." I'd carried it in my red vinyl wallet.

Whenever my teachers told me I'd never make it to college, I'd take it out and study it, repeating its promise softly to myself.

I'd believed that verse, even when my teachers kept saying, "With all the school you've missed, Roberta, you can never catch up." Perhaps they felt it was kinder not to let me dream too much, because I was afflicted with neurofibromatosis, a serious neurological disorder.

"Why, Roberta dear, come in, come in," Mrs. Withers's voice sang out. "I need a million and one things. I'm so glad you came to see me."

Gingerly, I eased myself onto the spotless white sofa and unzipped my tweed satchel, filled with all the cosmetics samples five dollars could buy. As soon as I handed Mrs. Withers a sales brochure, I felt like the most important girl in the world.

"Mrs. Withers, we have two types of creams, one for ruddy skin tones and another for sallow skin," I explained with newfound confidence. "And they're great for wrinkles, too."

"Oh good, good," she chanted.

"Which one would you like to try?" I asked, as I started to adjust the wig hiding my stubbly, surgery-scarred scalp.

"Oh, I'll surely need one of each," she answered. "And what do you have in the way of fragrances?"

"Try this one, Mrs. Withers. They recommend that you place it on the pulse point for the best effect," I instructed, pointing to her diamond-and-gold–clad wrist.

"Why, Roberta, you're so knowledgeable! You must have studied for days. What an intelligent young woman you are."

"You really think so, Mrs. Withers?"

"Oh, I know so. And just what do you plan to do with your earnings?"

"I'm saving for college. I want to be a registered nurse," I replied, surprised at my own words. "But today, I'm thinking more of buying my mother a cardigan sweater for her birthday. She always goes with me for my medical treatments, and when we travel on the train, a sweater would be nice for her."

"Wonderful, Roberta, and so considerate. Now what do you have in the gifts line?" she asked, requesting two of each item I recommended.

Her extravagant order totaled $117.42. *Had she meant to order so much?* I wondered. But she smiled and said, "I'll look forward to receiving my delivery, Roberta. Did you say next Tuesday?"

I was preparing to leave when Mrs. Withers said, "You look absolutely famished. Would you like some tea before you go? At our house, we think of tea as liquid sunshine."

I nodded, then followed Mrs. Withers to her pristine kitchen, filled with all manner of curiosities. I watched, spellbound, as she orchestrated a tea party, like those I'd seen in the movies, just for me. She carefully filled the tea kettle with cold water, brought it to a true boil, then let the tea leaves steep for exactly five minutes. "So the flavor will blossom," she explained.

Then she arranged a silver tray with a delicate china tea set, a chintz tea cozy, tempting strawberry scones and other small splendors. At home, we sometimes drank iced tea in jelly glasses, but never had I felt like a princess invited to afternoon tea.

"Excuse me, Mrs. Withers, but isn't there a faster way to fix tea?" I asked. "At home, we use tea bags."

Mrs. Withers wrapped her arm around my shoulders. "There are some things in life that shouldn't be hurried," she confided. "I've learned that brewing a proper pot of tea is a lot like living a life that pleases God. It takes extra effort, but it's always worth it.

"Take you, for instance, with all your health problems. Why, you're steeped with determination and ambition, just like a perfect pot of tea. Many in your shoes would give up, but not you. And with God's help, you can accomplish anything you set your mind to, Roberta."

Abruptly, my journey back in time ended when the lady in the hot, sticky attic asked, "You knew Hillary Withers, too?"

I wiped a stream of perspiration from my forehead. "Yes . . . I once sold her some of these cosmetics. But I can't understand why she never used them or gave them away."

"She did give a lot of them away," the lady replied matter-of-factly, "but somehow, some of them got missed and ended up here."

"But why did she buy them and not use them?" I asked.

"Oh, she purchased a special brand of cosmetics for her own use." The lady spoke in a confidential whisper. "Hillary had a soft spot in her heart for door-to-door salespeople. She never turned any of them away. She used to tell me, 'I could just give them money, but money alone doesn't buy self-respect. So I give them a little of my money, lend a listening ear, and share my love and prayers. You never know how far a little encouragement can take someone.'"

I paused, remembering how my cosmetics sales had soared after I'd first visited Mrs. Withers. I bought my mother the new sweater from my commission on the sale, and I still had some left over for my college fund. I even went on to win several district and national cosmetics-sales awards. Eventually, I put myself through college with my own earnings and realized my dream of becoming a registered nurse. Later, I earned a master's degree and a doctorate.

"Mrs. Withers prayed for all these people?" I asked,

pointing to the dozens of time-worn delivery bags on the table.

"Oh, yes," she assured me. "She did it without the slightest yearning that anyone would ever know."

I paid the cashier for my purchases—the sack of cosmetics I'd sold to Mrs. Withers and a tiny, heart-shaped gold locket. I threaded the locket onto the gold chain I wore around my neck. Then, I headed for the airport: Later that afternoon, I was addressing a medical convention in New York.

When I arrived in the elegant hotel ballroom, I found my way to the speaker's podium and scanned the sea of faces— health-care specialists from all over the country. Suddenly, I felt as insecure as on that long-ago day, peddling cosmetics in that unfamiliar, affluent neighborhood.

Can I do it? my mind questioned.

My trembling fingers reached upward to the locket. It opened, revealing a picture of Mrs. Withers inside. I again heard her soft but emphatic words: "With God's help, you can accomplish anything you set your mind to, Roberta."

"Good afternoon," I began slowly. "Thank you for inviting me to speak about putting the 'care' back in health care. It's often said that nursing is love made visible. But this morning, I learned an unexpected lesson about the power of quiet love expressed in secret. The kind of love expressed not for show, but for the good it can do in the lives of others. Some of our most important acts of love, sometimes, go unnoticed. Until they've had time to steep, time for their flavor to blossom."

Then, I told my colleagues the story of Hillary Withers. To my surprise, there was thunderous applause. Silently, I prayed, *Thank you, God; and thank you, Mrs. Withers.*

And to think, it all began with a perfect pot of tea.

Roberta Messner

Bacon and Eggs

Some friends play at friendship but a true friend sticks closer than one's nearest kin.

Proverbs 18:24

I was standing underneath the doors that led to my high school's gymnasium, music blaring, the stands packed with family and friends. I was waiting anxiously to make my entrance and had mixed feelings. This was it. The moment I had long awaited.

"Are you nervous?" someone asked behind me.

I turned around and saw the brown corkscrew curls of Beth Ann, my old friend from elementary school.

"Yeah, kinda. It just feels so weird," I said.

"Yeah, I know. It seems like yesterday we were playing line soccer and 'Bacon and Eggs' at recess," she said with a reminiscent smile.

"Bacon and Eggs," as we called it back then, was a game we played every day at recess. It involved two people on different swings locking their arms and legs together as tight as they could, and other people pushing them from all directions to try to break them apart. No matter how rough the ride seemed, Beth Ann and I never let go. We were inseparable.

Someone's hand reached out and nudged me along. It was my turn to walk. As I rounded the corner, all I could see were thousands of people and all I could hear was "Pomp and Circumstance." I had heard the song a dozen times before, but this time it had meaning. It seemed to take over my whole body, and my heart seemed to beat along with the notes. Tears filled my eyes as I realized that this was the last time I would ever walk with my friends. I marched underneath the flowered arches and turned down the aisle to my seat. When I sat down, I took a deep breath and took in everything around me—the people yelling and waving; my heart still beating with the song; all of my old elementary school friends in their caps and gowns; the class banner. The banner read: "The end of a decade, a century, a millennium, the beginning of a dream." At that moment, I realized that it was finally time to live the dream I had been planning for years. This was it. This was the moment I was to grow up and become the person I wanted to be. On the other hand, it also meant leaving everything behind.

The ceremony was long, and hot—very hot. My gown was drenched with sweat and tears, and it made me itch. I went hoarse from yelling for my friends when their names were called, and my mouth ached from laughing at the teachers who, after four years, still mispronounced our names. I grinned from ear to ear as I received my diploma and saw Mom and Dad looking down at me with eyes of pride. And, of course, at every reference made toward this day as being our last, I cried. But I made it through to the end.

As I marched out of the gymnasium, I looked to the people who had impacted my life through the years—to the people who made my life worth living, the people I would always carry with me. I looked to my parents, my family, my teachers and, finally, to my best friend from elementary school.

Through the years the group of us had grown apart, and we had all gone our separate ways. But Beth Ann was right. It seemed like yesterday we were playing in the school yard and dreaming of high school, which seemed, at the time, to be forever away.

I remembered the time Beth Ann and I were sitting outside on the stoop that led to our elementary school doors. We had just finished a game of hopscotch and were throwing rocks across the parking lot.

"I can't wait till we're in high school," I said, while wiping the sweat off my forehead.

The sun was hot and beating down on my toes. I was wearing my new hot-pink Jelly shoes that I had begged my mother for weeks to buy.

"I can't either. And when we get our license, we can drive to each other's houses and go to the movies or swimming anytime we want," Beth Ann rambled on.

"I know. I can't wait. We'll go everywhere together . . . we'll always be together," I promised.

"Best friends forever!" Beth Ann said.

"Yeah . . . best friends forever," I nodded.

We sat on that stoop planning out our future together— the places we'd go, the things we'd do and the people we'd marry. We planned on getting married at the same time to best friends just like us. We planned on teaching our kids to play "Bacon and Eggs," and to teach them how to never let go.

As I walked out of the gymnasium, I remembered all the plans we had made in elementary school. I realized that none of them had come true. But there was a place in my heart that still wanted them to become reality. In the back of my mind, even after all the years apart, I had secretly hoped we'd always be together.

I followed the long line into the cafeteria to meet my family and friends. I received thousands of hugs and took hundreds of pictures. I was pulled in a million directions, but I was still remembering my elementary school days with Beth Ann, the promises we had made and the plans we had dreamed up when we were young. I had to say good-bye.

I searched for her through the crowd. I looked for ten minutes, and when I was about to give up, I turned the corner and there she was, surrounded by a bunch of people. I walked over to her and pulled her to the side.

"Beth . . ."

We called her "Beth" now because she felt that she had outgrown "Beth Ann."

" . . . I don't know what to say. I guess I just felt like I had to come over and say good-bye."

At that last word "good-bye," she pulled me into her arms and gave me a big hug. We held on to each other for what felt like hours but was probably only a few moments. When we pulled away, we both had tears in our eyes.

She whispered to me, "I just want to thank you for the memories. I love you. I'm gonna miss you . . ." She was staring into my watery eyes and gripping my fingers so tightly they were turning purple. "I'll never forget you."

"I'll never forget you . . ." I repeated, as I slowly let my fingers slip away. I was finally able to let go. I turned and walked away.

I walked through the high school doors that night by myself, with my thoughts dashing around in a hundred places. I realized as I walked out that I was beginning a new life—a life without my elementary school best friends, a life of new friends and new connections, and hopefully a life of "Bacon and Eggs" with friends who can hold on as tightly as Beth Ann could.

Beth Dieselberg

One More Task

Eve Jesson could have been bitter, but an inner strength—and her faith—sustained her. She had been widowed at seventy, after forty-three busy years as a minister's wife. Then she had a stroke at age seventy-four, which affected her entire left side: Her left hand and arm were weak, and she walked haltingly with a four-pronged cane. Nevertheless, her mental ability was sharp, and her independent spirit was strong.

Her daughter urged Mrs. Jesson to join their household, but she gently refused. "I don't think it works out for the best," she said, "but I'd love to visit you often." She sold her home, distributed her most precious possessions among family members and moved into a nursing home where I was a caregiver. She soon became a joy to all of us on the staff. She was fastidious, thoughtful and friendly. She took part in activities, helped arrange flowers and did a bit of "mothering" here and there.

It was difficult for us to find her a suitable companion to share the two-person bedroom. Many of our residents had severe health or personality problems, or were mentally infirm. With a quiet, gentle manner and the ability to do things for herself, Margaret Gravelle seemed like a

more suitable roommate than many others. While
Margaret's memory was vague, she knew she was ninety
years old and had spent her life in nursing. Her only relative was her great-nephew.

Although Mrs. Jesson made few complaints about it, we
knew Margaret woke her several times in the night when
she was confused about sounds or the bathroom location.
Mrs. Jesson had to remind Margaret of mealtimes and guide
her to the dining room. Margaret could not grasp the notion
that only one of the closets was hers and the other was for
her roommate. One day a nurse aide brought Margaret
back into their room to change her blouse from the one of
Mrs. Jesson's she was wearing, to one of her own.

"Well, she does have good taste," Mrs. Jesson said wryly.
"That is my new silk blouse I got for my birthday."

A day came when we had arranged for the admission of
a lady we thought would be a better companion for Mrs.
Jesson. "I think we can provide a more suitable roommate
for you in a couple days," I told her. "We just have to
arrange to move Margaret to a different room."

Later in the day, Mrs. Jesson came down to my desk.
"Don't move Margaret," she said. "She really needs someone to look after her. She gets anxious in the night. She has
no family and she is used to my being there.

"You know, I asked God many times why I had to go on
living. When John died, I felt as if my life was finished too.
But family, friends and faith all helped me. Then I had my
stroke and I thought, *Why damage me so and let me go on living?* Well, maybe he had work for me yet. Maybe I'm
meant to look out for Margaret. I can give her some of the
comfort my family gives me. Leave her in my room. It
won't take that much effort to watch over her a bit."

Leaning on her cane, that gracious lady started back
down the hall to her room to carry out the last loving task
he had given her.

Marian Lewis

5

UNEXPECTED FRIENDS

*How rare and wonderful is that flash of a
moment when we realize we have
discovered a friend.*

William Rotsler

A Friendly Act of Kindness

Friendship is the golden thread that ties the heart of all the world.

John Evelyn

Beverly and I have been best friends for years, and, like a well-worn sweater, our friendship has hung in there, through thick and thin. After her divorce three years ago, she moved several states away. We keep in touch through cards, letters and weekly telephone calls. Her call last Saturday night changed both our lives.

When the phone rang, I could almost predict who'd be on the other end. I picked up the receiver and said, "Hello?"

"Hello, yourself," a meek voice answered.

"Beverly, how are you doing?" Silence.

"I found a lump in my breast," she whispered, at last.

A chill ran down my spine. "Are you sure?" I imagined the usual bright stars in her eyes flickering, then fading in reflection of her terror.

"Have you seen the doctor?" I bit my lower lip.

"Yes. The biopsy report came back positive. It's

malignant," she sobbed. "I'm scheduled for surgery on Tuesday."

I tried to reassure her, but I knew she was terrified, and so was I. I did my best to hide my own fears. We chit-chatted some more, struggling to avoid the subject. After we hung up, I told my husband, who agreed I should book a flight. After all, I couldn't let Bev face her uncertain future alone.

The next two days and nights dragged. Monday morning finally arrived, and I drove the long trek to the nearest airport. Even with the heavy traffic to distract me, my thoughts kept returning to Bev. I prayed the whole way. The old belief, "C=D" (cancer equals death), kept creeping into my mind. I'd lost my mother to that disease seven years ago.

When I arrived, I wrote down where I parked and wheeled my bags to an open elevator. Exiting on the ticketing floor, I waited in line for about twenty minutes until it was my turn to step up to the counter and hand my identification to a tall brunette.

Her fingers tapped the computer keys for a moment. She studied the screen. When she looked up and handed my identification back, she said, "I'm sorry to inform you this flight is currently overbooked. If you can come back tomorrow morning, we can accommodate you on another flight."

"But," I stammered, "I have to get on this flight. This is not just a vacation trip or anything like that. My best friend is having surgery—she needs me." A tear formed and trickled down my cheek.

"I'm sorry. Everyone showed up, which is usually not the case. Even the standby passengers aren't getting on."

"But I made a reservation."

"Yes, just two days ago. That's why you've been bumped." She shrugged her shoulders and said, "Next."

I trudged away from the counter and plopped into a vacant seat to assess my situation. All the while tears streaked my face. I fished in my purse for a tissue, dabbed my cheeks and blew my nose. The loudspeaker announced the first boarding call for rows twenty to thirty. I watched several people rise and hurry to obtain a place in line. I swallowed hard. A sinking feeling in my chest turned into a knot as it reached my stomach. Defeated, I sighed and bent down to gather my bags.

"Perhaps I can help you," a soft voice said. "I couldn't help overhearing your conversation with the reservationist."

I glanced up and saw an older woman with smiling blue eyes gazing at me. The early morning sunbeams streaming in through the large airport windows illuminated her ivory complexion. Soft silver-gray hair framed her face. I wiped away a tear and asked, "How?"

"Well, I have a ticket and am assigned seat 7B. I'd be honored if you would take my place." She waved the ticket and boarding pass at me. Her intense eyes seemed to beckon me to take it.

Tempted, I hesitated for a moment, wondering what the catch was.

"I couldn't take your seat. Aren't you anxious to get to your destination?"

Her smile faded. "There's no one waiting for me at the other end. I live alone. Staying here one more day won't make a difference. My daughter will come and take me back to her house. Won't my grandchildren be surprised?"

I could almost taste her loneliness. I said, "It would mean so much to me. But I'd never be able to repay you. Are you sure?"

Her eyes sparkled. "Don't be silly. Go to your friend." She handed me the ticket.

Humbled by her kindness, I accepted. We strolled to the counter together and made the necessary changes.

Because of her compassion, I would be able to be with Beverly and to give her my love and support. Gratitude flooded my soul.

I turned to this generous mystery lady and extended my hand. She took it, squeezing back, and said, "Someday you'll see a woman in distress and you'll do the same." With a wink, she released my hand.

My trip was a success. Everything went well with Beverly: The surgeon assured us both that he'd removed all of the cancer.

To this day, I often think of that special woman who sacrificed convenience for friendship. I will never forget her act of kindness. I hope when it's my turn, I can give as freely as she did and pass on her legacy of kindness.

Suzanne A. Baginskie

The Other Woman

In the oddest way, though hardly in the traditional way, she was "the other woman," the dangerous mistress/seductress/threat/rival. She was accomplished, bright, sensible, sensitive and altogether charming.

So why did I so automatically and reflexively resent her the moment I heard about her? Why did I mind terribly that she was all those things . . . and unspeakably thin, to boot?

I minded because Ruthi was to be our youngest daughter Nancy's "other mother," the mother she was inheriting through her marriage to Ruthi's son Michael.

And as wonderful as that was—as thrilled as we were that Nancy had found a man who truly made her feel whole and special and loved—there were still early anxieties.

The most terrifying change: Nancy would no longer be connected to just one mother. Ruthi—the other woman—would share our beloved Nancy with her father and me for the rest of our lives. And that notion definitely took my breath away, along with some of my confidence.

"So . . . what is Michael's mother like?" I had asked Nancy with studied nonchalance when they first met.

"Oh, she's great!" Nancy had responded without missing a beat. "You'll love her!"

Hmmmm.

Later: "So . . . what does Ruthi do?"

The mere mention of her high-powered glamour job that carried with it the title of president made me weak with insecurity.

Still later: "So . . . what does Ruthi look like?"

Okay, so I regard myself as an enlightened woman who knows that appearance is superficial, that the book must not be judged by its cover. But you can bet I still winced when Nancy went into a glowing description of Ruthi's perfect coif, her megawatt smile, her luminous skin. And it did bother me a bit that Nancy's future mother-in-law has trouble fitting into anything larger than a size four. . . .

Over the months, now years, that followed, Ruthi and I have had our own "courtship." Initially reserved, even timid, with one another, we have moved through the awkward phase of blind date/first meeting, that exploratory stage of getting a read on one another. And in our case, we have reached the gloriously triumphant stage of discovering that, yes, we *do* share values and many of the same ideas about what makes life meaningful and rich.

I gained a new and very dear friend in the very woman I saw as such a terrible threat. I have a pal, a confidante, a buddy in the generational alignment, one who understands why I am so madly in love with our mutual grandchildren—three adorable, fierce little boys who have, of course, drawn our families even closer.

I've long since gotten past the tricky moments that came in a pummeling stream early in this "marriage" between two women.

No longer do I pout when Nancy decides that Ruthi's recipe for lemon-baked chicken has mine beat by a mile.

Years ago, that would have made me feel vaguely threatened. Would Nancy decide that Ruthi's brownies and sour-cream coffee cake were also superior? My whole maternal culinary record had been suddenly called into question, and I never even prided myself on my cooking.

"I'm pouting over a chicken recipe," I had told my husband, with astonishment. And we both knew in that instant that chicken recipes—or recipes for brownies or coffee cake—were really not the issue at all. The issue felt more like . . . betrayal.

Not anymore.

There are weeks when I talk to Ruthi more than I talk to my daughter. There is a new tradition of spending New Year's Eve with one another and our respective adult children. It's wonderful!

There is one powerful common denominator that unites Ruthi and me: We are mothers who love our children, and our new grandchildren, beyond all reason. Before we ever met one another, we shared that incredible link. We both have known the pleasure of memorizing a child's face, of gulping in his or her first word, or standing in the silent dark and watching a son or daughter sleeping, and realizing that there is no more beautiful sight on God's earth.

Ruthi and I remember when this son and daughter were huggable creatures who planted carrot roots in paper cups and chocolatey kisses on their mothers' cheeks at bedtime.

So of course we had strong motivation to become friends. But too often, that motivation flags in the face of rivalries, personality clashes and who knows what else.

Ruthi and I know that even though the rabbi who united Nancy and Michael in holy matrimony did not mention uniting their mothers, a different kind of union has formed: our own.

I feel blessed that "the other woman" has become a caring friend.

I feel enormously grateful that out of this whole wide world, our children found one another.

And so did we.

Sally Friedman

And a Little Child Shall Lead Them

Little friends may prove great friends.

Aesop

The setting was a McDonald's restaurant in a small community in central Pennsylvania. Most of us think of dining at McDonald's as "fast food." Not so for a lonely, retired eighty-year-old woman, whose physical and mental health was waning. Each day, she arrived early in the morning and sat at a back booth until late afternoon, seeking companionship and hoping to be included in the conversations of nearby patrons.

June was her name, and home was a second-floor apartment in the nearby college town. Despite the steep steps that were becoming increasingly difficult for her, the pleasant ambience of McDonald's drew her to the corner she called her "home away from home." Each day this proud woman sat bundled up in the same back corner, wearing a familiar babushka on her head, her eyes always hidden behind dark sunglasses, her heavy coat buttoned.

During the fall of 2001, my four-year-old granddaughter,

Catie, attended preschool three days a week; I picked her up each day at the sitter's and took her to lunch before I dropped her off at school. Most children love "Mickey D's," and Catie was no exception! Catie's favorite seat was one table away from June on the same bench seat.

I must admit I became tired of eating hamburgers, and I would often ask Catie, "Could we please go somewhere else today?" Her answer was always an adamant: "No, Nana, I have to see June." Each day as we approached the parking lot, Catie's eyes would search for June's battered 1975 Monte Carlo, with the cluttered interior containing June's "treasures." When she spotted June's car in the handicapped space, she was elated. As soon as I got her out of her car seat, she would race ahead of me, bounding through the restaurant, craning her neck to see if June was in her spot. If she was, they played a little game. Catie would pretend to hide behind a display, peek around the corner, then race into June's arms. Many patrons watched for Catie and smiled tenderly as this adorable little blonde child clasped her friend tightly, proving to all that friendship transcends age. As I reflect on this relationship, I realize that God planned for these two to meet and to bond.

Over the months, Catie would bring June small gifts: a key chain from her first trip to Disney World, a bouquet of flowers hand-carried to her apartment when June was sick, a mug for her birthday with a photo of Catie perched on June's lap in their favorite corner of McDonald's.

Unfortunately, in the fall of 2002, just as Catie entered kindergarten, June's health deteriorated to the point where she had to have dialysis treatments three times a week. Many days, her seat would be empty when we arrived at McDonald's. Catie always asked one of the clerks about her friend. Sometimes, the manager or one of the workers, who had also befriended June, would give us an update. Near Christmastime, Catie and I received the news that June had gone to a nursing home.

When we first found June's room, she was lying in bed with her eyes closed. June seemed to sense our presence, and, as her eyes opened, she spotted Catie. Catie walked over to the bed, June sat up and they hugged. Tears filled my eyes as I realized the power of the moment. They talked a mile a minute, and June showed Catie the bird-feeder outside her window. This visit was a ray of sunshine for June, whose life was far from sunny. Her diabetes was worsening; her beloved car had to be sold; and the outlook for the future was bleak.

Before we left that day, June opened Catie's Christmas present, a pink fleece blanket to keep June's feet warm. She loved it, and they hugged tightly once again. Over the next few months, school kept Catie busy, yet each time we went to McDonald's, Catie's eyes were drawn to that back corner.

Before Easter, I received a phone call from a McDonald's employee telling me that June's health was failing; they were going to have to amputate her leg. Catie sent a card to June, telling her she would pray for her. Soon, we got even worse news: June had passed away.

Catie would be in school on the day of June's funeral, but we sent two pink roses with some babies' breath. The morning of the visitation, I walked into the funeral home to pay my respects. Only two small flower arrangements were visible, and the people there were few. As I walked down the aisle, a woman who identified herself as June's niece approached me, wondering who I was. When I told her that I was the grandmother of Catie—June's friend from McDonald's—she grabbed my hand and led me to the casket. There lay this peaceful angel with her white babushka on her head and with Catie's two pink roses in her hands. I soon learned from her niece that roses had been June's favorite flowers. The pink fleece blanket covered her legs, and on top of the blanket were Catie's card and the photo of the two of them in the corner booth at McDonald's, Catie sitting on June's lap and June resplendent in her trademark dark glasses and babushka. Tears flowed from my eyes. In that moment, I truly came to see what a gift God had given the world in my grand-daughter, whose genuine love had wholly embraced this lonely, elderly woman.

While taking Catie to school the day of June's funeral, we talked about my saying good-bye to June for her. She asked me about the memorial card that was lying on the seat next to me. I read it to her, and we talked about their birthdays both being in June, but that this year, June would be in heaven for hers. As she got out of the car, she wondered if she could take the card to school and I told her that was fine. She bounded up the sidewalk with her friend Carly, who asked her what she had in her hand. I heard her explain, "This is my best friend, June."

Audrey Conway

An Arm for a Friend

Lots of people want to ride with you in the limo, but what you want is someone who will take the bus with you when the limo breaks down.

Oprah Winfrey

The doorbell downstairs rang again. My Vicodin-induced daze slowed me down significantly, and I was still several steps away from the buzzer that unlocked the main door in our apartment complex.

Every little move was killing me. Too weak to lift my good arm, I just leaned against the buzzer. It buzzed and buzzed. Somewhere deep down my subconscious registered the hurried steps up the staircase, my apartment door opening and a blonde head appearing.

"Good job, darling," the blonde head smiled as she gently put her arms around me and led me back to the couch. Was this Victoria or Anna?

I couldn't tell. Since my accident and the subsequent surgery, everything was a blur. I was aware that there was a constant stream of visitors through my apartment, but I did not realize until later, when I got better, that my girl-friends tag-teamed to take care of me.

Just a few days before Christmas, on our way to a ski vacation, our Jeep hit black ice and rolled over. Miraculously, all of us—my newly married friends, their dog and I—survived the accident. The only serious injury any of us sustained was a shattered left arm—mine.

After a series of emergency helicopter rides, various hospital stays and a lengthy surgery, I finally stood a good chance of a full, but very long, recovery.

Back in San Francisco, with lots of titanium in my arm and still taking an enormous amount of painkillers, I arrived at the apartment I shared with Stacey, a very nice woman whom I barely knew. I had recently moved in with her on the recommendation of a friend of a friend, and although we liked each other, we each led busy lives and ended up spending very little time together. Stacey was one of the few people whom I actually informed about my accident, as I didn't want to cause a panic among my friends.

Little did I know, in my hazy state, that upon my arrival she would quickly assess my situation—and with the skill of a trained disaster-response professional, act smoothly and firmly.

"She will be staying in my room," she instructed David, my doctor friend who drove me home from the hospital and was the only other person aware of my misfortune. "My bed is higher than hers, so it's easier to get in and out of."

Too dazed to understand what was going on and too weak to complain, I was led into her room and helped into her bed. I quickly fell asleep.

As it was later recounted to me, Stacey sat David down, questioned him about my state and my needs, and made him promise to call our closest mutual friends to ask them to get in touch with her. She also called all my girlfriends whose numbers she could find in my little notebook by the phone. In a couple of days she had a very efficient little operation going.

Because my family lived thousands of miles away, Stacey and my girlfriends divided up all the duties, making sure that I was never left alone for too long.

Stacey took most morning and evening shifts. She was also the one who did my shopping and laundry, and who gave me a sponge bath every other day.

Friends with flexible schedules would come by and check on me during the day; others would cook for me or take me out to get some fresh air or just simply keep me company.

Still, I spent most of my time with Stacey. She rearranged her social schedule so her friends came over more often; or if they went out, she would plan a night at the movies so I could join them. I was extremely grateful to her, even though I felt very uncomfortable having to rely on her—an almost total stranger—for all my basic needs. Somehow, this awkwardness rapidly disappeared. As the oldest of four siblings, taking care of others came easy to Stacey. She and I connected on many levels—it turned out that we had not only almost identical backgrounds, but also many interests and values in common. We really liked each other's friends as well, so spending time together was a pleasant change, rather than a distraction, for both of us.

Fully recovered now, my life is completely different from my life before the accident. I changed careers, and now I spend more time on my hobbies and with my friends—especially Stacey. Although my injury took a lot out of me, it also made me reassess my priorities and gave me a great friend who has become a cornerstone of my new life.

Monika Szamko

The Nicest People I Never Met

Many people believe that we have to actually meet people for them to be real friends. I highly disagree. My three girlfriends are the nicest people that I have never met. They live in various places in the United States. One lives in the sunny state of California. Another lives in the great state of Texas, while the third lives in Illinois.

I have known each of these ladies for several years, but never met even one of them. We discovered each other online, formed close relationships through e-mail, and have shared our hearts by telephone, snail mail, and through instant messages.

Approximately five years ago, I met Kathy. She read a story that I wrote and posted online. My story was so similar to her own life story that she had to write to me. We hit it off instantly and became wonderful friends. She, like me, is a freelance writer. We share all our accomplishments. We express our writing concerns to each other and we cry over rejections.

When I have good news, I cannot wait to write to Kathy. Likewise, when I have bad writing news, I cannot wait to share it with her, as well. I know she will make me feel better with her encouraging words and comments. If we don't receive an e-mail from the other every day, we both become concerned.

Diana was the second girlfriend I met online. We, too, have been communicating for several years. Again, Diana read a story I wrote and had published online. As a result, she wrote to me. Diana sent baby gifts when my grandchildren were born. She has never forgotten one of my birthdays or any other holiday, as far as that goes. I collect frogs. Diana has added many to my collection. I think of Diana every time I hear my frog wind chime as it dances in the breeze.

Diana telephoned me numerous times following my husband's open-heart surgery. After my surgery, two years later, she outdid herself. For the entire six-week recovery period, I received a card from her almost every day. On the days I didn't receive one, I had two in my post office box the next day. I saved every card. I also cherish the love that she sent along with them. Diana loves me so much that she wanted to make me smile through the pain I was feeling.

Annettee is the third girlfriend that I met online. She, too, read one of my published stories and contacted me. She is a writer, as well, so she understands the ups and downs that I feel while pursuing my writing career. Annettee and I don't miss many days talking on the telephone. Some days we find ourselves spending entire afternoons together in conversation.

While talking, we discuss issues that are important to each of us. Inspirational messages, spiritual insights and family happenings are among our most talked-about subjects. I have grown spiritually and became a better person because of her friendship.

Friends may not always be people we can see face-to face. We cannot always reach out and hug our friends or physically wipe away the tears from their eyes. We cannot sit together and share a cup of coffee or shop together until we drop. While it would be wonderful to be able to meet each of my girlfriends one day, we all know that because of the distance between us, we have to simply use modern technology to help our friendships grow for the time being.

I am thankful for the stories that I have written over the years that caught the attention of my three online girl-friends. I do not believe that our friendships could have been any better if we lived just a few miles apart. I am thankful for the Internet and the opportunity to meet three friends who have made my life so much better.

A true friend is available when you need her. My friends have been there for me through thick and thin. All I had to do was go online or dial a telephone number when I needed any of them. Because of our unique relationships, I am convinced that even friends we have never met can and will be our friends forever.

Nancy B. Gibbs

An Anonymous Rose

"Happy Valentine's Day," one of the other teachers called to me as we left the school building and walked to the parking lot.

"Thanks, the same to you."

She giggled as I returned the greeting. "This will be the most romantic Valentine's Day ever. Burt and I were looking at diamond rings, and he asked what kind I wanted. I'm sure he's going to propose tonight."

"Congratulations," I said. "Although I should congratulate the groom and say 'best wishes' to you."

"Maybe you better save it, in case I misread the signs." Even though she smiled, I saw the panic in her eyes.

"There's no school on Saturday and I can't wait until Monday," I said. "Call me tomorrow with the happy news."

"Okay. If you don't hear from me, you'll know the news was bad."

"It'll be good," I assured her with a thumbs-up sign.

I watched the young teacher burn rubber as she took off. She was so in love and so eager to start her romantic evening, I felt for her.

Dear Lord, I whispered, *please make this a happy day for her to remember, not a disappointment. May she receive the proposal and the ring she wants, and may their love last forever.* Then I added, *Please help me through the pain of remembering my own special Valentine's Day.*

Ray and I had dated for years and were deeply in love, but a lot of obstacles kept us from marrying. Finally, the time was right, and, though we couldn't have a big wedding, we wanted it to be special.

"Let's get married on Valentine's Day," I told Ray. "Even with your absentmindedness, you won't forget our anniversary."

Miraculously, Ray never had a problem remembering our anniversary. Of course, the valentine cards I always scattered over the house for weeks ahead might have helped.

For our twelfth anniversary we invited our two closest couple friends to dinner, and Ray brought me a dozen long-stemmed red roses. "One for each perfect year," he'd written on the mushy valentine enclosed.

That was the last anniversary we ever celebrated. Ray died eight months later.

The date I chose so he would remember, became a day I would come to wish to forget. But I never could. Worst of all, now I was alone on Valentine's Day every year.

My children were grown and married. My actor buddy was rehearsing a new play, and I could no longer count on Mary, my frequent companion. There was no romance on the horizon, no small grandchild to give me a handmade, crayon-drawn paper heart. Because I was a reading specialist and didn't have a regular class, I had no handful of "teacher" cards.

Thoughts of going home to a lonely, empty house were so depressing, I stopped at the mall. Nothing captured my attention, and I wandered around in a daze. Enticing smells wafted to me as I passed a large restaurant, which reminded me that I was hungry, but I didn't have the guts to go in by myself. I considered going to the movies, but again, I couldn't face going alone.

Feeling there was no place left to go, I went home. The house was dark as I pulled into the driveway, but the automatic light came on as I approached the house. I gathered the mail from my mailbox, and clutching it in one hand, opened the storm door with the other.

On the step between the doors was a long, slender package wrapped in green tissue: I could hardly wait to open the wrapping.

Once inside the house, I unwrapped the paper to reveal a single perfect, long-stemmed red rose. Its beauty and sweet scent reminded me of the dozen red roses Ray had given me so long ago. I tore through the wrappings looking for the card, but there wasn't one. I looked for a clue to the sender's identity, but came up empty-handed.

After a while, I called my son and daughter, but neither of them knew anything about the rose. "You must have a secret admirer," my son said. "There's a guy out there who's interested in you."

My daughter's explanation was less encouraging. "The florist may have delivered it to the wrong house."

"There was no address on the package," I told her. "It must have been left in person."

"Then it was probably a neighbor—someone who wanted to thank you for a favor."

The possibility sounded logical, and I racked my brain trying to decide if I had done anything special for one of my neighbors. When nothing came to mind, I began to mull over my son's suggestion. I had to admit, the idea of a secret admirer intrigued me. Being a romantic at heart and having a writer's imagination, I spent the rest of the evening weaving all kinds of plots around the idea. In fact,

I became so absorbed, I didn't remember this was a day I'd wanted to forget.

I never did learn who brought me the rose, but I knew it had to be a good friend. A friend who cheered me by letting me know someone cared, yet wise enough to give me something to wonder about.

Since then, starting with the young teacher who didn't get the hoped-for proposal, I've given an anonymous rose to many friends in pain. I hope each one has brought as much comfort as the one that I received brought me.

Polly Moran

The Red Coat

The squares and triangles for the quilt are poured across her lap like jewels. Patches of golds, greens, reds. She runs her hand over a block of garnet-red wool and smiles.

It was a cold, windy day, with winter nipping at the heels of fall. She picked up Abby from grade school and they rode the city bus downtown. Abby was bundled in a hand-me-down coat from her cousin, Linda Sue. It was perfect, with a rabbit fur collar, and hardly worn. They hopped off the bus and she held Abby's hand as they dashed across the street. The wind whipped up a piece of newspaper and cut right through her thin brown coat— the same coat she'd gotten just before the war. Styles had changed a lot since then, with hemlines going up and down like an elevator. Now there wasn't enough of the coat left to alter, and her full skirt peeked out from beneath it like a dust ruffle.

John had been home since September, and the only job he'd been able to secure was as a janitor at the hospital. He hoped to start night school in January; education seemed to be the ticket to a better job. Lately, he'd scrimped and saved, and just that morning handed over twelve dollars, saying, "Now, you go over to Harricks and find yourself a good winter coat." She'd agreed, thinking it would be a challenge to find much of a coat for twelve dollars. She knew he meant well, but it might have been better to put the money under the mattress for a rainy day. Lord knew they'd had plenty of those.

As she and Abby entered Harricks, she suddenly remembered how she used to shop there with her mother, back when money flowed freely, before she'd married John against the wishes of her family. Now the shop seemed like a foreign land, and she felt like an intruder.

"May I help you?" asked a plump woman straightening gloves in a glass display case.

"No, thank you. I just want to look around a bit." No use telling her she was looking for a coat, with only twelve dollars in her purse. The woman might laugh.

She walked through the store, pretending to observe the many pretty things. Abby pointed out a peacock blue evening dress. "That would look nice on you, Mommy." She stroked her daughter's sleek brown hair, the same color as her own, and smiled. Finally, they reached the back of the store and she turned around, ready to give up. Relief mixed with disappointment. But nestled in the corner was a rack with various items, the sign above it proclaiming: "Sale." She glanced at the rack and something red caught her eye. It turned out to be a wool coat in a lovely shade of red, just the color of garnets. She carefully removed the hanger from the rack and searched the coat for a price tag. But surely, even on sale, it would cost too much.

"Mommy, the tag says twelve dollars!" Abby triumphantly held up the sleeve with the bright yellow tag. "You can get it, Mommy! That's just the right price."

"Oh, that can't possibly be right. It's much too nice. There must be some mistake."

"Try it on, Mommy. See if it fits." Abby tugged at the sleeve of her old coat.

"It's probably not even my size." But in the same moment, she lay down her old coat and slipped into the red coat. She couldn't explain why, but it felt like honey. It was delicious.

"It's perfect, Mommy. And it's beautiful! You look like a princess." Abby pushed her toward the mirror. It looked fine, probably too fine. And perhaps the red, though lovely, was too bright for a woman almost thirty. She hung the coat back on the hanger, then held it at arm's length to study it again. It was a nice design, with bound buttonholes and large abalone buttons. Even the lining was smooth heavy satin—that's why it felt like honey.

"Are you going to buy it, Mommy?"

"Oh, I don't know, Abby. I think there's a mistake. This is a very well-made coat. The price tag can't be right. Coats like this don't end up on the clearance rack, especially in November."

"It says twelve dollars; it must be right." Abby folded her arms and tapped her little foot with impatience. "Daddy said you're supposed to buy a coat. Now you better get it."

She smiled down at Abby, then put the coat over her arm and headed for the counter. An elderly woman was being waited on. The sales clerk carefully placed a brown felt hat with a long black feather into a hatbox and rang up the price. The cash register jingled as the tray popped open.

"That'll be thirty-two dollars," announced the clerk, and the woman wrote out a check without even blinking. She picked up her pretty box and bid the clerk good day.

"Can I help you?" asked the clerk sweetly. Her hand was extended as she reached expectantly for the coat.

"No, I, uh, I think I'd like to look around just a little

more." She stepped back and studied the coat again. The price tag was a mistake. If a silly hat sold for thirty-two dollars, how could this beautiful coat be twelve?

"What are you doing, Mommy?" complained Abby as she followed her back to the sales rack.

"Honey, I just know it's a mistake. You can't buy a coat like this for twelve dollars. There's no point in even asking. We'll just look silly."

"But the tag says—"

"Shhh, honey, don't make a scene." She looked around.

Several other shoppers were close by now. She recognized Lily Andrews from church. She was new in town, and her husband was a doctor. Mrs. Andrews smiled in their direction and moved toward the sales rack. It seemed strange that someone so well off would be interested in clearance items. Her hand paused on the red coat and she pulled it from the rack.

"May I help you?" asked the clerk.

"What a lovely coat. And only twelve dollars?"

"That's right. It was from last year; someone returned it in July, if you can believe that. A woman kept it all winter and never wore it. She never even took the tags off. The store owner just wanted to get rid of this coat since it doesn't fit with the new line up in front. It's quite a bargain—"

She couldn't hear any more. She took Abby's hand and quickly led her out.

"But Mommy, that's your co—"

"Shh, honey."

Tears stung her eyes as the wind blew even colder outside. It was still too early for the return bus, but they settled down on the bus stop bench to wait, anyway, huddling together for warmth.

"Why didn't you get your coat, Mommy?" Abby's voice was sad.

"I don't know, honey."

How could she tell her it was because she was foolish? And not only was she foolish, she was too proud to ask. How could she explain to John that their eight-year-old daughter had more sense than she did. She shivered. She deserved another winter in her old worn-out coat. That would teach her a lesson!

"Excuse me," called a voice. She looked up to see Lily Andrews.

"Yes?"

"I know this is going to sound very strange. And believe me, I don't usually do things like this, but I just got the strongest impression to give you this. I have no idea why." She thrust the package toward them.

"I don't understand—"

"Neither do I. But it's as if God told me to do this. I know it's very strange; you probably think I'm crazy."

"It is strange." She peeked in the bag. "I almost bought this coat just a few minutes ago. Please let me pay you for it." She grabbed eagerly for her purse.

"No, that's just it. I got the impression I was to give it to you. You cannot pay me for it. I'm sorry. I must sound like a madwoman. . . ." Her face was red, and tears were in her eyes.

"But I can't take this; it's like charity."

"No, it's not charity. Go ahead and give your money to someone who needs it if you like. But I know I'm supposed to give this to you. I'm sorry if I sound nutty; maybe I'm just lonely, but it's the first time I ever thought I heard God tell me to do something. You have to let me do it. Think of it as a gift from God . . . an act of faith."

That was more than four decades ago. She'd worn the coat for many winters. Finally, it was so out of style that even Abby pleaded with her to give it up, but she could never bring herself to part with it. It had been packed in a trunk for ages, and she'd only thought of it last week when Dr. Andrews passed away and she wanted to do something special for her friend Lily. Now she was carefully cutting the pieces into a lap quilt for her good friend. She hoped it might be a comfort and a reminder that faith can be found in small things like red wool coats . . . and enduring friendships.

Melody Carlson

A Gift from Ute

Driving down I-95, I could not believe where I was going. It was a Saturday morning in September 1991 when the phone rang, and I was informed that my dear Ute had been struck down by a hit-and-run driver while out for her early morning run. She was in a coma and it didn't look as if she was going to pull through.

I was in a daze when I arrived at the hospital and found her husband in a family waiting room amongst some friends I vaguely recognized. Waiting in the hall was Ute's best friend, Linda. We had met a few months earlier at a surprise birthday party Ute had given for her husband.

Ute didn't have many female friends. Most women were intimidated by her extraordinary beauty, never giving themselves a chance to know she was equally beautiful on the inside. Linda had been Ute's best friend for twenty years. I met Ute while both our sons were attending the same boarding school in New England. It was not long before Ute and I created a powerful bond and friendship.

Now, in the hospital corridor, Linda and I embraced and cried as if we were the oldest of friends. The next week was a nightmare for everyone, with daily vigils that drew us closer to the inevitable. Friday, the family made the heart-renching decision to disconnect Ute from life support. One week earlier, Linda and I barely knew each other and now we were walking hand in hand, blinded by our tears, down a long hallway to say our private good-byes to our dear friend. As Ute's final moments went by, bells began going off throughout the hospital. It was a surreal moment, almost as if everyone should be made aware of our loss. The world, just at that moment, had lost a human being of extraordinary grace and dignity. The ordeal was over.

The friendship between Linda and me could have ended right then and there, but the most amazing thing happened: During the weeks that followed, we found ourselves calling each other every day, sometimes twice a day. We would comfort and support one another through our disbelief that Ute was gone. We were of one mind and heart.

We made time in our schedules to see each other, often going out to dinner with our husbands, Herb and Hal. We soon discovered we both had the same white dishes, the same sheets, the same coffee mugs and the same toaster with the ugly red knobs. We both were artistic and creative, loved animals and beautiful things. Most of all, we loved Ute.

As time went by, the four of us took a cruise together, enjoyed each other's families, celebrated holidays and events together, and carried on a tradition that began many years earlier between Ute and Linda and their husbands. Every year, we would spend New Year's Eve together, just the four of us, no matter what.

Linda and I have forged a rare bond, closer than two sisters. Our identical sense of humor keeps us laughing for days. We are extremely trusting and protective of one another, like the comfort of a warm blanket. Linda is at the center of many friendships. Each and every friend feels blessed and honored to be counted as part of her life. She has helped me to be able to tell the important people in my life, "I love you," something I used to find difficult to do.

We both lead busy lives. I am a designer of handcrafted art cards, with a studio in my home. Linda, a psychiatric nurse, went back to school at age forty-one to get her doctorate in psychology. While Ute was there for most of the years of school and study, I was there for the culmination. On that joyous graduation day, sitting in the audience among Linda's family, Ute was there, too.

Five years later, tragedy struck again. Our dearest Hal developed cancer and died within seven weeks. Linda was left without her soul mate of thirty-one years. There were times that I felt so helpless, as my heart broke for her and her two wonderful sons. But I knew I was helpful by just being there whenever she needed me.

The day before Hal died, an unbelievable thing happened. Linda, after arriving home from the hospital that evening, began sorting through the day's mail. Among the various envelopes, she came upon a piece of junk mail advertising an upcoming seminar. As she was about to discard it, she stopped in total confusion. The mail was addressed to Ute but at Linda's address. Ute's address was crossed out and Linda's address was crudely scrawled in, in pencil, and in a most unusual, almost primitive, handwriting. How was this possible and what did it mean? Never, in five years, had Linda ever received mail addressed to Ute. We all were shocked and bewildered, and realized by the next day, after Hal's death, that there was only one explanation: This was Ute's way of letting us know she was there, waiting for Hal.

As if this phenomenon was not enough, it would seem that Ute had to be absolutely certain we understood. While getting ready for Hal's funeral, Linda's sons suggested that they put a picture of Ute into Hal's coffin, along with other meaningful memorabilia. They searched through whatever photographs they could find and came up with only one. Stunningly, it was a long forgotten one of Ute, smiling brightly, holding a huge balloon that said, "Welcome Home." We knew our friend was so close that we could almost reach out and touch her. She certainly was touching us.

The joy of Ute's friendship did not die. Instead, it lives on in the treasured relationship that Linda and I now share. Throughout these past six years, we have grown to value each other more and more, never once taking our friendship for granted and always realizing it evolved through very unique circumstances. We hold our friendship in the highest regard and are both entrenched in the belief that the love, respect and joy we bring to each other's lives would never be possible without this "Gift from Ute."

Wendi R. Morris

The Angels on the Cruise

My husband, Mike, and I lost our soon-to-be eleven-year-old son in a gun accident on December 7, 1993, shortly before his birthday. The journey down the road of grief is very exhausting, and there are many days you don't think you can keep going. We had to keep going; we still had our thirteen-year-old daughter, Jayme, depending on us—besides, Sean would not have wanted us to give up. Many times remembering his jokes and laughter and feeling his love got us through some very rough moments.

Even through the pain, we have had many blessings come to us on our journey through grief. One of these blessings occurred during the Thanksgiving of 1994. Thanksgiving had always been a special time for our family. We liked being together, just the four of us. We would take turns cooking our favorite dishes, have a relaxing dinner, decorate the Christmas tree, light the tree when the Plaza lights were turned on, then sit around and eat appetizers while we enjoyed the tree. So that Thanksgiving the three of us needed to have a "different" Thanksgiving holiday. Mike had always wanted to go on a cruise and we thought that might get us through our "first"

Thanksgiving. When someone you love dies, you remember things in your life as two parts: before they died and after they died. It's like you're starting a whole new life whether you like it or not.

People think you can get away from your grief by taking a trip, but for those of us going through this journey of grief, you know the pain always goes along. So you have to do the best you can. I did a lot of praying about going on this cruise, hoping it would take a little bit of the edge off the pain.

We got lucky on the cruise: The weather was great and on the second day, on a tender boat going to Key West, we met three really nice people from Orchard Lake, Michigan. It's funny how, when you don't bring a friend along for your daughter, you're always looking around to see if anybody has a daughter, preferably the same age, to hang out with. As luck would have it, Denise Falzon found us first. We all seemed comfortable with each other and agreed to meet later that evening back on ship.

Chris and Denise's daughter, Nikki, was six months older than Jayme, and they had everything in common—from being on student council to being in musicals—except losing a brother. The girls had fun together. The big day arrived and we were out at sea all day. We spent the day on deck with Chris, Denise and Nikki laying out, relaxing and talking. Denise had asked if I had any other kids and I told her no, just Jayme. I guess I didn't expect to see them again or I would have told them. We met for a show later in the evening and I remember looking at the Falzons with envy, thinking *If they only knew of the pain we are carrying* and wondering what it would feel like to just be "normal" again.

We enjoyed the time we spent with the Falzons, and at the end of the cruise we exchanged addresses and said we would write to each other.

A couple of days after Christmas, I received their Christmas card in the mail. As I began to read the card, I started to shake. Denise thanked us for helping them get through another holiday. Their nineteen-year-old son, Brian, had died October 1, 1993, collapsing at his college campus from sudden arrhythmia. So now, Nikki and Jayme *were* just alike; they both had had a brother who had died suddenly.

With over two thousand people on board that ship, we had met another family who also had lost a son and around the same time—almost as if our sons had matched us up.

I knew the Falzons were spending Christmas out of town, but I hurriedly wrote them a letter about Sean and sent a picture to them. I wanted the letter to be waiting for them when they got back from their trip. They were shocked and called as soon as they read our letter. We just talked and talked—and we're still talking six years later. Denise and I are a mini-support team for each other around the anniversaries of our sons' deaths.

This year Sean would have been graduating from high school, so we are planning a trip to visit Chris and Denise during graduation weekend.

I think being thankful for our blessings no matter how small and reaching out to help someone else, especially when we are feeling down, has been a tremendous help to Denise and me and our families. Opening our hearts to the love around us helps us to still feel the love of our sons. Love has no boundaries.

Shari Dowdall

Lavender Memories

I know that the world is not filled with strangers. It is full of other people—waiting only to be spoken to.

Beth Day

As Cotha Prior strolled past the new shop that sold body lotions and soaps, the lavender-wrapped bars displayed in the window caught her attention. Her daughter, Monica, would like those. Once inside, Cotha picked up the closest bar and held it to her nose. The fragrance carried her back to her childhood.

She remembered Margie, the little girl in her fifth-grade class who always was poorly dressed and whose bathing habits were, well, not one of her regular habits. Even at that young age, Cotha knew how important the opinions of her friends were, so although she felt sorry for Margie, she couldn't risk being friends with her.

Then one afternoon, as the young Cotha colored the states on her homework worksheet, she casually mentioned Margie to her mother, who stopped in the middle of stirring the stew to ask, "What's her family like?"

Cotha didn't look up. "Oh, really poor, I guess," she answered.

"Well, it sounds as though she needs a friend," Mrs. Burnett said. "Why don't you invite her to spend Friday night with you?"

Cotha looked up quickly then. "You mean here? Spend the night with me? But, Mom, she smells."

"Cotha Helen." Her mother's use of both names meant the situation was settled. There was nothing to do but invite Margie home.

The next morning, Cotha hesitantly whispered the invitation at the end of recess, while her friends were hanging up their jackets and combing their hair. Margie looked suspicious, so Cotha added, "My mother said it's okay. Here's a note from my mother to give to yours."

So two days later, they rode the school bus home, while Cotha tried to ignore the surprised looks on her friends' faces as they saw the two of them together. Have two fifth-grade girls ever been quieter? Cotha thought of other times when she'd been invited to spend the night with a friend. They would talk and giggle all the way to their stop.

Finally, Cotha gave a determined little huff and said to Margie, "I've got a cat. She's going to have kittens."

Margie's eyes lit up. "Oh, I like cats." Then she frowned as though recalling a painful memory and added, "But my dad doesn't."

Cotha didn't know what to say then, so she feigned interest in something outside the school-bus window.

Both girls were silent until the bus rolled to a stop in front of the white house with the green shutters.

Mrs. Burnett was in the kitchen. She greeted Cotha and Margie warmly, then gestured toward the table set with two glasses of milk and banana bread. "Why don't you girls have a little snack while I tend to dinner?"

When the banana bread was finished, Mrs. Burnett handed each child identical paper-doll books and blunted scissors. Dressing the paper women in shiny dresses gave them something in common to talk about. By the time they washed their hands for dinner, they were chatting enthusiastically about school.

After the dishes were done, Mrs. Burnett said, "Time to take a bath before bed, girls." Then she held out scented soaps wrapped in lavender paper. "Since this is a special night, I thought you might like to use fancy soaps," she said. "Cotha, you first, and I'll wash your back for you."

Then it was Margie's turn. If she was nervous about having an adult bathe her, she didn't show it. As the tub filled, Mrs. Burnett poured in a double capful of her own guarded bubble bath. "Don't you just love bubble baths, Margie?" she asked, as though the child bathed in such luxury every day.

She turned to pull Margie's grimy dress over her head, then said, "I'll look away as you take the other things off, but be careful climbing into the tub. That brand of bubble bath makes it slippery."

Once Margie was settled into the warm water, Mrs. Burnett knelt down and soaped the wet washcloth heavily before rubbing it over the child's back.

"Oh, that feels good," was all Margie said.

Mrs. Burnett chatted about how quickly Cotha and Margie were growing and what lovely young women they were already. Repeatedly, she soaped the washcloth and scrubbed Margie's gray skin until it shone pink.

Through the whole thing Cotha was thinking, *Oh, how can she do that? Margie is so dirty.* But Mrs. Burnett continued to scrub cheerfully, then washed Margie's hair several times. Once Margie was out of the tub, Mrs. Burnett dried her back and dusted her thin shoulders with scented talcum. Then, since Margie had brought no nightclothes, Mrs. Burnett pulled one of Cotha's clean nightgowns over Margie's now shining head.

After tucking both girls under quilts, Mrs. Burnett leaned over to gently kiss them good night. Margie beamed. As Mrs. Burnett whispered, "Good night, girls," and turned out the light, Margie pulled the clean sheets to her nose and breathed deeply. Then she fell asleep almost immediately.

Cotha was amazed that her new friend fell asleep so quickly; she was used to talking and giggling for a long time with her other friends. To the sound of Margie's gentle breathing, Cotha stared at the shadows on the wall, thinking about all her mother had done. During Margie's bath, Mrs. Burnett had never once said anything to embarrass the girl, and she'd never even commented about how grimy the tub was afterward. She just scrubbed it out, quietly humming the whole time. Somehow, Cotha knew her mother had washed more than Margie's dingy skin.

All these years later, the adult Cotha stood in the fragrant store, the lavender soap still in her hand, wondering where Margie was now. Margie had never mentioned Cotha's mother's ministrations, but Cotha had noticed a difference in the girl. Not only did Margie start coming to school clean and pleasant on the outside, but she had an inside sparkle that came, perhaps, from knowing someone cared. For the rest of the school year, Cotha and Margie played at recess and ate lunch together. When Margie's family moved at the end of the school year, Cotha never heard from her again, but she knew they had both been influenced by her mother's behavior.

Cotha smiled, then picked up a second bar of the lavender soap. She'd send that one to her mother, with a letter saying that she remembered what her mom had done all those years ago—not only for Margie, but for Cotha as well.

Sandra Pickelsmer and Bobbie Valentine

6

OVERCOMING OBSTACLES

*Whether you are blessed with soul mates . . .
Or with those who walk with you just a
little while, not one of these friends crosses
your path by chance. Each is a messenger,
sent by God, to give you the wisdom,
companionship, comfort, or challenge
you need for a particular leg of your
spiritual journey.*

Traci Mullins

The Book of Friendship

Happiness isn't the easiest thing to find, but one place you're guaranteed to find it is in a friend's smile.

Allison Poler

December 24 arrived along with heavy snow that clung stubbornly to the roads. Highways closed and the authorities issued travel advisories throughout the day. Into the evening it fell, sealing in the somberness of the day.

Let it snow, I thought. It was my first Christmas Eve without my mother, and my sadness dampened the day's usual excitement. Any excuse not to leave the shelter of my small apartment seemed good to me.

The telephone rang. I ignored it and went to my bedroom to bury my face in the softness of my pillow, hoping to muffle out the incessant and demanding shrill, knowing it must be my friend Rebecca calling. It was eight o'clock and I was supposed to be at her house for dinner.

I'm doing her a favor by not being there, I thought to myself. *How could I be joyful when I feel so lousy? I want to be left alone.*

My eyes were red and sore from the tears that would not stop. My heart felt as heavy as the falling snow. My grief was piled as high as the snowdrifts.

How do I stop missing my mother?

I must have drifted off to sleep, for I awakened with a start. Someone pounded at the front door.

I tiptoed to the window and looked through the frosted pane. Seeing Rebecca's car parked out front, I padded back to bed and drew the covers over my head.

"Girlfriend!" she shouted. "I know you're in there. Answer the door!"

"Leave me alone!" I shouted back.

The floorboards creaked in the hallway. I heard paper rustling as she slid something under the door.

"Merry Christmas," she called out.

Not answering the door made me feel worse, if that was possible. I wasn't being fair to my best friend. Ever since grade school, we had been inseparable. Most people mistook us for sisters. Her father and sister died in a car accident when she was eight years old. As a result, her mother had to return to work, and Rebecca was pretty much left to fend for herself. She became a fixture at our house.

Still, my misery kept me from answering the door.

When I was sure she left, I retrieved the small square package. Wrapped simply in gold foil, it had no other decoration. Carrying it to the bench by the window, I sat down and unwrapped it: a gold pen and a journal. When I opened the front cover, out fell a bookmark with a note on it:

Dear Sister Friend,
   My words won't heal the pain. But your own words can.
Love,
Rebecca

I stared at the blank pages, not wanting to spoil the pure whiteness with empty phrases. A single tear fell and the page absorbed it. I wrote my name on the first page and looked at it for a long time.

Out of the corner of my eye, I caught some movement on the windowsill outside. A cat sat crouched, waiting to pounce on a sparrow that just landed in search of some seed I sprinkled there earlier in the day. Every time the cat pounced, the sparrow flew away, returning only moments later to eat the rest of the seed. I am a terrible artist, however, to my bewilderment, I sketched several pictures of the bird, as it flew away and returned again. Next I drew the cat, poised and ready to attack its prey.

When the cat finally gave up on the sparrow and darted to another ledge, I surveyed my drawings.

Am I the sparrow or the cat? I wondered. I wrote the question beside the drawings, then closed the journal.

Over the following months, my stormy emotions took refuge within the pages of the book. Tears fell on the paper as often as words.

Prayers tearfully written, faith renewed. The storm ebbed as each image and word touched the pages.

I was the sparrow, foraging for answers and oblivious to the threat of being swallowed by grief.

As my heart healed, so did my understanding of the incredible friendship Rebecca and I shared. This journal was, in essence, an extension of her friendship. Even though I pushed her away at a very difficult time, she found a way to help me communicate my grief, by giving me this "surrogate" friend.

One night, I picked up the phone and dialed her number.

"Looks like the snow is melting," I said.

Spring was just around the corner.

S. A. (Shae) Cooke

Big Problems, Little Miracles

A true friend loves at all times—good and bad.

Proverbs 17:17

My pastor called it my "midlife crisis." Personally, I think it was just a string of rotten luck, including horrendous income changes, my son's poor health winging its way into its sixteenth straight month, medical bills that could choke a buffalo, bewilderment following cross words with two of my grown children, the empty-nest syndrome looming just months away when my youngest would be leaving for college eighteen hundred miles away, daily lower back pain due to lack of exercise, arguments with a woman in Texas over a book we were co-authoring and the fact that I'd only seen the sun for about twenty-six hours all winter.

Call it any old psychobabble thing you want—midlife crisis, midwinter funk, too many lifestyle changes at once, mild depression, premenopausal angst, seasonal affective disorder or simply being sick of being a single parent after twelve years. Whatever it was, the fact remained that I was not my usual cheerful self from the end of January until mid-March that year. By then my friends and family had caught on that the big-time blues had invaded my home, heart and health.

For a time, it was all I could do to barely take care of the three basics around the house: food, clothing and shelter. For about a week, during the bleakest days of all, the smallest things could reduce me to tears. I bit my lip a lot, trying to hold back tears.

One day after a job interview, I stopped at my friend Sharon's house for a cup of tea. She knew something was wrong, even though I didn't go into all the details. She hugged me, poured a second cup and tried to make me laugh. As I was leaving, Sharon noticed one of the two buttons that hold the decorative belt on the back of my winter coat was missing, causing the belt to dangle ridiculously in the back.

At that moment, during that extremely low point in my life, I honestly could not comprehend how or when I would manage to sew that button back on. Mortified, I felt hot tears sneaking into my lower lashes as I headed for the front door.

Sharon pulled open my coat at the bottom. "Hey, look here. There's an extra button sewn inside. Take your coat off and I'll sew it on for you right now."

At that moment, I felt more love and more compassion from a friend than ever before in my life. Granted, over the years, my friends have been wonderful to me, with me and for me. But this gesture, when I was at such a state emotionally, dragging so low that a missing button was about to send me over the edge, the gift of Sharon's time, her caring and intuitive knowing that I could not muster the energy to sew that button on myself, meant more to me than if someone had come to my door with a sweepstakes check.

When I got home that afternoon, I found a silly greeting card in the mail from another friend, Kay. Inside, it simply said, "I've got a hug here with your name on it." Every time I looked at that card for the next couple of weeks, I felt loved and buoyed by the light of Kay's friendship.

A few days later, on what was probably the darkest day of all, a day I seriously considered begging my doctor for a Prozac prescription, my Texas coauthor, the one I'd had arguments with as we worked on our book, sent me a "sunshine box." Little miracles of love spilled out of that box: chocolates, red silk tulips, sunflower candles, ginger-lily bath gel and three little juice boxes of pure Florida gold.

My heart melted as I noticed for the first time that day that the sun was actually shining. I took one of the juice boxes and the candy out to the deck and sat in my favorite yellow rocker in the forty-degree weather, sipping juice and basking in the glorious sunshine and in the wonderful miracle of friendship.

That sewed-on button, the hug card and the sunshine box got me through those dark days without drugs or further mental deterioration.

And when I began taking brisk half-hour walks every morning the following week, I did a lot of thinking about those friends of mine and their gifts of love. Before I knew it, I understood one of the most amazing, most profound aspects of life: God has designed the world and his people in such a way that no matter how big our problems, the smallest gesture given in love from a friend can become the biggest miracle of all.

Patricia Lorenz

The Necklace

Be slow in choosing a friend, slower in changing.

Benjamin Franklin

During the winter of my sophomore year of high school, I counted the days until summer vacation. Regardless of "the count," I still dressed for school, tested my blood, took my shot, ate, ran out the door and headed to my first-period class. It had been a difficult year for me. Being at a new school is challenging for most kids. It didn't help having to monitor my diabetes and live with other health-related issues. Regardless, I tried to attend class four periods a day and met with a home schoolteacher twice a week. This gave me a full class load.

The highlight of my day was choir class. There I felt accepted. Half the girls in the choir were typical; the other half was made up of girls with special needs. Though our looks and abilities varied, we all loved lip gloss, new clothes—and, of course, singing.

One day, each of our class periods ran short, so the entire school could gather at the amphitheater for the

Holiday Wish Fairy Assembly. For a moment, the only wish I had was that I was back at the Christian high school I had attended my freshman year. How I wished that it hadn't had to close!

Because I had never been to a Holiday Wish Fairy Assembly before, I had no idea what to expect. I sat back and waited for it to be over. The assembly began with announcements, and then the "wishing" part began. One by one, members of the ASB cabinet called various students up onstage. Each student made a wish. One wished for a car; another, a dog. The dreaming went on and on.

What a dumb assembly! I thought.

Soon, all eyes were on Elizabeth, a girl from my choir class. *What's she doing up there?* I wondered. *For a girl with special needs, she sure has guts!*

Elizabeth stepped in front of the microphone. Without a tremble in her voice, she began to talk. "My wish today is that I could give Jenna Mitchell a present in front of the school."

Jenna Mitchell? That's me! My heart began to pound.

Within seconds, a member of the ASB announced, "Would Jenna Mitchell please come up to meet Elizabeth?"

Without thinking, I rose to my feet and began the long walk to the stage. With the entire school watching, I smiled at Elizabeth, then stood by her side.

Elizabeth began the short monologue that she had rehearsed several times. "I want to thank Jenna for being my best friend at school, and I want to give her this necklace."

Extending her hand toward mine, Elizabeth gave me a small gold box tied with a matching ribbon. As the students watched, I thanked Elizabeth and gave her a hug.

With tears in my eyes, I returned to my seat. Then, I realized I did have friends at my new school. I also had a "best friend"—one who understood how it felt to be different, who knew what it was like to have special needs and who loved to sing as much as I did.

Jenna Mitchell

Melts in Your Heart, Not in Your Hand

Though she had been in a coma for nearly six months, it was still a shock when my grandmother passed away. She'd had her third stroke the year before and had lapsed into the silent sleep afterwards, leaving her family to sit by her bedside at the hospital, to ache, to cry and to pray. I was not yet thirteen when she died, and the first thing I clearly remember was the shock that she was gone forever. I'd understood that death awaited her, but in those first moments of knowing, I could not believe that "eventually" had finally come to pass.

What was to follow was the pomp and circumstance of a typical Catholic send-off. First, there would be wakes. Four of them. Two on the first day, one from 2:00 P.M. to 5:00 P.M., and one from 7:00 P.M. to 9:00 P.M. The same schedule would be repeated the following day. The third day would be the funeral itself, the church funeral, then the final burial at the graveyard. It seemed like too much to take. For the next few days, my whole life would become death: staring at the body of my grandmother amidst the overwhelming scent of too many fresh flowers, feeling the eeriness of the funeral home and dreaming of her at night, her ghost hovering over me while I tried desperately to fall asleep. My real life, the life of an eighth-grader who was almost done with grammar school and off to high school, had never seemed farther away.

At the funeral home, friends and neighbors poured in to pay their last respects to my grandmother and to show support for my mother. Not knowing where to be or what to do, I stayed off to the side, not wanting to upset my mother. The awkwardness finally came to an end, with the arrival of my friend Kelly.

She lived down the street; we'd been friends ever since she was three and I four. My mother had been so pleased when she discovered that a family with a little girl had moved in down the street—finally, a playmate for me! She and Kelly's mother, Patti, became fast friends, as did Kelly and I. Though I was a year older than her and we were in different grades in school, it didn't matter much. We were "home" friends, the kind that rode bikes together after school and made up plays for our Cabbage Patch kids to act out. When we got older, we grew more mischievous and began sneaking to a diner a few blocks away for ice-cream sundaes, even though we weren't allowed to leave the block. When finally we were allowed to leave the block, we'd go around the corner for pizza, but stopped first in the alleyway to put on pink lipstick and eye shadow.

At the funeral home, Kelly's parents went to the coffin and knelt to pray. Kelly came right to me. In her hands were two packages of M&M's, original and peanut. Kelly knew that candy was one of my favorite things; we had often taken long trips to the local store for chocolate bars and lollipops. "I thought this would make you feel better," she said. For the rest of that wake and the others that Kelly attended, we sat in the back of the viewing room, eating M&M's and talking quietly. A devastating and unfamiliar experience had suddenly become easier to bear, with a childhood offering of chocolate candies and the company of a devoted friend.

When my other grandmother passed away two years later, Kelly was there once again for all of the wakes and the funeral, and came bearing M&M's for each one. It's a difficult thing, trying to come up with something to offer a grieving person . . . what do you do for a person who has just lost one of the most important people in their lives? Kelly had understood, even at twelve, that there wasn't much she could do to ease my pain but be there with me and bring something that just might make me smile. When Kelly's grandmother died a year after that, I arrived at her wake with a one-pound bag of M&M's.

Now, whenever Kelly and I find ourselves at a funeral home for a family member of ours, the other has always shown up bearing M&M's, a small offering of cheer to take the edge off the hovering sorrow. We've joked that when we're old, whichever one of us dies first will have a crazy old lady throwing M&M's into her grave, while the other mourners will look on in confusion. It's a silly thought, but M&M's will always be significant to me now. They will remind me that even when something as painful and as powerful as death comes to claim what's most important to me, there will always be chocolate . . . and Kelly.

Jennifer Stevens

My Best Friend

Not many may know the depths of true sisterly love.

Margaret Courtney

I was always jealous of my big sister, Ellen. She was the pretty one. She was the popular one. She was the friendly and generous one who could do no wrong. I truly believed that "Mom always liked her best." Did I feel any different than any other kid sister? Probably not. But when she gave my parents their first grandchild, a beautiful blue-eyed, golden-haired girl named Jillian, I was convinced that I could never be as good as she.

From the day she was born, Jillian owned my heart and my thoughts.

I was only an aunt, yet I felt as proud of her as if I were her mother. I never knew that it was possible to care so deeply for another person. The greatest thing about our relationship was that we could enjoy all the pleasures of an aunt-niece friendship without the authoritarian role of parent getting in the way. I loved her and I laughed with her, but I never had to get angry with her for not doing her homework or fighting with her brother. What a smug look I must have had on my face when we were in public together and people assumed that she was my child.

Jillian once said, "You are so cool, Auntie Benita, so different from my mother." I treasured those words, yet inwardly, I felt guilty that her own mother could not experience the unconditional love that Jillian and I shared. There were no expectations, no demands, no obligations . . . just the pure satisfaction of being together.

When Jillian was an infant, she was diagnosed with cystic fibrosis. My sister greeted the news with resolve and with a strength that was unyielding. At first the CF didn't have much of an impact on Jillian. Sure, she coughed a lot, but that never stopped her from having a regular childhood, even though everyone assumed that her cough meant she was sick with a cold. There were many times when parents on the playground or in school would chastise Ellen for putting their children in contact with Jillian's germs. Most times, Ellen would not feel like explaining that the cough came from a lung disease and not the flu.

There were many rocky moments throughout the years. When Jillian did get a cold, it was never simple. Sometimes, oxygen masks were necessary. Other times, hospital stays were involved. Visits to the doctor were almost as frequent as trips to the grocery store. And, oh, those blood tests! Every diagnosis, every doctor's appointment, every little sneeze seemed to require a blood test that Jillian hated—passionately. She would scream and kick and try to run away. Anything to not have a blood test. No amount of cajoling or bribing could get her to readily submit.

Except for me. If I was there, it was somehow better. She still protested, but not as loudly or as vehemently.

As the illnesses and the accompanying absences from school became more frequent, it became clear that Jillian was not like every other kid. Ellen never wavered in her determination to not give in to the CF. Jillian should not be singled out as needing special attention, as being different. On her good days, Jillian could do whatever little girls do—go to school, play hopscotch or Barbie. Sometimes, she would tire easily, but that did not stop her from being smart, sociable and busy.

As Jillian got older, our relationship got even better. She confided in me things that she would not tell her mother. This made me feel very special.

When I walked into the room, her face would light up and she would yell, "Auntie Benita," as if just my being there was better than any medicine. I think it might have made Ellen a little jealous. That was okay. In some distorted psychological way, it was my revenge against my older sister just for being an older sister and for always being better than me. Now, I was in a position of strength. I had something that she wanted—her daughter's confidence.

Childish emotions aside, Jillian was our connection. Ellen and I didn't have much in common until Jillian came along. Now we saw each other often and spoke on the phone regularly. We were forming an adult relationship and playing a much larger role in each other's lives. Jillian was the focus of our conversations and attention, as we shared the events of her life together.

And then Jillian's condition started to deteriorate. Her hospital stays became lengthier and more frequent. It was scary when she was very ill, and we all sat around somberly thinking the worst but not admitting it. No one ever mentioned the inevitable, but in our hearts, we had to accept it as a reality.

I watched my sister grow old and tired before my eyes. The physical and emotional strain was eroding her strength but she never gave up hope. I don't know how she did it: Looking into Jillian's eyes knowing that she would never grow to adulthood. Realizing every morning that the end was just a little bit closer, but never giving up hope. Her attitude remained positive, even though there was little reason for optimism. I came to realize that the sister I envied had become my hero.

The only way I can make any sense of Jillian's death is to believe that things happen for a reason. Ellen wants to know what reason could be important enough to require her child to die. Jillian brought us closer together and forced us to share our happiness, our strength and our sorrow.

A bond was formed far stronger than anything we had ever known. We came to truly love and respect each other. I'm not sure if that would have happened had it not been for Jillian's life . . . and death. That is certainly not a good enough reason for a child to die, but God works in mysterious ways. All I know is before Jillian was born, I had a big sister. Now, I have a best friend.

Benita Baker

Good Morning, Sunshine

There are no good-byes for us. Wherever you are, you will always be in my heart.

Mahatma Gandhi

I didn't sleep well that night. I tossed and turned, dreading the next day. Somehow, I knew that my friend's test results wouldn't be good. I woke up early that morning and took a quick shower. As I turned off the water and heard the telephone ringing, I raced to the phone and so I was given the dreadful news while still soaking wet. I just stood there dripping both water and tears.

"Good morning, Sunshine," Doris said. She hesitated for a few moments, then announced, "It has come back, honey. The cancer is back." I knew that I had to be strong for Doris. My mind began to race, as I thought about all the things that she had done for me. "You're the only one I've told, honey," she added.

"I'll be there shortly," I promised.

I had met Doris six years earlier. My husband and I accepted the pastorate of the small country church where she was a member. Because of her bright smile, Doris instantly won my heart. Doris was old enough to be my mother, but I had never had a friend quite like her before.

While driving to the hospital, my memories took me back to the days right after we met. My father was diagnosed as "terminal." Doris called me every day once the diagnosis was made. "Good morning, Sunshine," she said many times over the telephone. Even though most mornings didn't seem very bright, her calls made me smile. Many times, Doris came to visit. She brought little gifts to cheer me up.

Because my father resided in a long-term care facility almost seventy miles away, I was exhausted. I worked two jobs, taught a Sunday school class and visited with Daddy several times a week. Many times my cell phone rang while I was driving home on the interstate.

"Good afternoon, Sunshine," Doris would exclaim. "Stop by my house on the way home. I have dinner prepared for you." I knew exactly what that meant. There would be an entrée, two or three vegetables, corn bread and a coconut pie awaiting me.

Once I arrived at the hospital, I tapped on her door and heard a faint, "Come in." As I opened the door, I saw my friend lying there in the bed. She smiled at me.

"Good morning, Sunshine," she whispered. "Thanks for coming." The room was dark. Even the flowers that we had taken to her the day before looked sad. I leaned over her bed and embraced her. We held each other tight and sobbed in each other's arms. Initially, there were no words. What do you say to a dear friend when you know that she will be leaving you soon?

"I love you, Doris," came out quite naturally. "I'm going to be with you through this," I assured her. "You can count on me."

Doris cried for a few seconds before she finally told me

what was bothering her. "I'm worried about leaving you, honey," she confided. "I want you to be okay." My dear friend was dying but was more concerned about my comfort. I assured her that I would be fine, but that her absence would leave a great void in my life.

For several hours that day, we talked about how we would break the news to her other family members. We discussed final arrangements, her pain medication toward the end and other important matters. The next few weeks were a blur. Between the many doctor visits, making sure she had plenty of food and fluids in the house, and keeping her prescriptions straight, we spent a great deal of time together.

One Sunday morning, I woke up early and called to check on her. I could tell that she needed medical care immediately. I rushed her to the emergency room. She was admitted that day and never returned home.

During the week preceding her death, I went to the hospital four to six times a day. I read the Bible to her at night until she fell asleep. Some mornings, I arrived even before she awakened. She lost her strength, but she never lost her beautiful smile. Each morning, I was greeted with her typical "Good morning, Sunshine." As I watched her grow even weaker, I wondered how many more mornings I would have the privilege of hearing those special words.

One afternoon, I received a call. "Doris has taken a turn for the worse," I was told. "You need to come." The doctors were trying one more procedure that would help to relieve some of the pain that she was experiencing.

"Can I speak to her alone for a second?" I begged the doctor as soon as I arrived.

"Sure," he said. Everyone left the room and allowed me to spend a few moments with my friend.

I took Doris's weak hand and held it tightly. We prayed together. "I love you," I told her.

"I love you, too, Sunshine," she whispered.

"There's nothing else we can do," the doctor announced to me after the procedure. I knew I had to break the news to her.

I walked from the hallway where I'd waited for the doctor back into Doris's room. "Did the procedure work?" Doris asked.

"I'm sorry, but it didn't," I answered and began to cry.

"Everything is going to be okay," Doris promised. "Please don't cry." The room was quiet for a few moments. Doris reached up and took my hand. "You don't know how much you have meant to me over the last few years. You made my life complete," she whispered. A few minutes later, Doris fell fast asleep.

The next morning, I went to see her as usual. Doris was obviously in severe pain and could no longer speak. Before the doctor gave her the strong medication that would ease her pain, I prayed with her and asked her if she knew that I loved her. She nodded. About that time the sunlight burst into the room as if to comfort my grieving soul.

That night Doris joined many of her loved ones in heaven. As I had promised, I was sitting by her side.

The next morning, I stepped outside and the August sun shone down upon my face. Its warmth made me think of Doris's unconditional love. "Good morning, Sunshine," I whispered as I looked up to the heavens. In my mind, I saw Doris's smile and knew that everything was okay just as she'd said. She had gone home.

Nancy B. Gibbs

The Love Squad

It is a good thing to be rich, and a good thing to be strong, but a better thing to be loved by many friends.

Euripides

"Oh, no! Not company!" I groaned, the moment my car rounded the corner and our house came into full view. Usually I'd be thrilled to see four cars lined up in our driveway, but after I spent a weeklong vigil at the hospital with an ill child, my house was a colossal mess. Turning off the car engine, I dragged myself to the front door.

"What are you doing home so soon?" my friend Judie called from the kitchen. "We weren't expecting you for another hour! We thought we'd be long gone before you got home." She walked toward me and gave me a hug, then asked softly, "How are you doing?"

Was this my house? Was I dreaming? Everything looked so clean. Where did these flowers come from?

Suddenly more voices, more hugs. Lorraine, smiling and wiping beads of perspiration from her forehead, came up from the family room where she had just finished ironing a mountain of clean clothes. Regina peeked into the kitchen, having finished vacuuming rugs and polishing and dusting furniture in every room in the house. Joan, still upstairs wrestling with the boys' bunk-bed sheets, called down her "Hello," having already brought order out of chaos in all four bedrooms.

"When did you guys get here?" was my last coherent sentence. My tears came in great heaving waves. "How come . . . how come . . . you did all this?" I cried unashamedly, every ounce of resistance gone.

I had spent the week praying through a health crisis, begging God for a sense of his presence at the hospital. Instead, he laid a mantle of order, beauty and loving care into our home through these four "angels."

"You rest a while, Virelle," Lorraine said firmly. "Here's your dinner for tonight—there are more meals in the freezer." The table was set with flowers and fancy napkins, and a little gift was at my place. A small banquet was arranged, complete with salad and dessert.

"Don't you worry; we're all praying," my friends said. "God has everything under control."

After my friends left, I wandered from room to room, still sobbing from the enormity of their gift of time and work. I found beautiful floral arrangements in every room . . . and little wrapped gifts on each bed. More tears.

In the living room I found a note under a vase filled with peonies. I was to have come home and found it as their only identity: "The Love Squad was here."

And I knew that God had everything under control.

Virelle Kidder

The Birthday Present

If we build on a sure foundation in friendship, we must love our friends for their sakes rather than for our own.

Charlotte Brontë

The minute Jenny and I got to the mall, I knew I shouldn't have come with her on this shopping expedition.

"My mom said she thought I'd have more fun shopping with you for my birthday present, so she gave me her credit card and told me to 'be reasonable,'" Jenny said, as we entered the clothing store.

I tried to smile at Jenny's remark, but I could tell my effort left something to be desired. I could feel my facial muscles tightening with forced cheerfulness as I imagined what "reasonable" meant. *You'll probably only buy three new outfits instead of five,* I thought, *and each one complete with shoes and other accessories.*

Before I could stop it, the green-eyed monster was rearing its ugly head.

Jenny and I had been best friends since the sixth grade.

Over the years, we'd done everything together—got short haircuts that we hated, discovered guys and complained about school.

At first, it never bothered me that Jenny's family was much more well-off than mine. Now that we were in high school, though, I began noticing the things Jenny had that I didn't—a fabulous wardrobe, her own car, membership at a fitness club. It seemed the list could go on forever. More and more, I was envious of her lifestyle and the things she had.

I couldn't help comparing this shopping extravaganza with birthdays in my family. We weren't poor, but four children in the family meant budgeting, even for birthdays. We had a good time, but my parents put a twenty-dollar spending limit on presents.

I remembered my last birthday. In our family, it's a tradition that the one who's celebrating a birthday gets to pick the menu and invite one special person to the celebration. I invited Jenny, of course, and ordered my favorite meal complete with chocolate cake for dessert. It was fun, but nothing like this credit-card shopping spree.

I was brought back to the present when Jenny held up a white sweater and matching skirt.

"Do you like this?" she asked.

"It is gorgeous," I said. Jenny nodded and continued looking while I moved from rack to rack, touching the beautiful clothes. "I'm going to try this on," Jenny headed for the dressing room. After a few minutes, she reappeared in the outfit she'd just shown me. She looked beautiful.

I sighed. While part of me wanted to tell her how good she looked, another part of me snatched the words back before they were uttered. Jenny was in such good shape that she'd look good in a potato sack. Sometimes, I doubted my judgment in choosing a best friend who was so pretty. *Lord, why can't I be the one with the rich parents and the great looks?*

"Well, Teresa, what do you think?" A question Jenny had asked me more than once. "Do you like it?"

The outfit looked great on her, but the green-eyed monster struck again. "Not really," I lied. "I think you need something with more color."

"You think so?" Jenny said doubtfully. "I don't know."

"Just trust me. We'll find something better," I told her pushing her back into the dressing room. "You just can't buy the first thing you see." I would have said anything to get Jenny out of the store and away from that outfit. As we left, Jenny gave the sweater one last look.

Just down the mall, we passed a frozen yogurt place. "My treat," Jenny said, pulling out her wallet. "The Taylors stayed out late Saturday night, so I've got a few dollars to spare."

I never could resist chocolate frozen yogurt, so we got our cones and sat down at a table. As Jenny chattered away about a million things, I thought about the feelings I'd had toward my best friend lately. Those feelings weren't very kind.

As I sat there, I began to see Jenny in a new light. I saw that Jenny was attractive not just because of her good looks, but more so because of her kindness. Treating me to yogurt was far from her only show of generosity. She took me to the fitness club she belonged to every chance she got. She also let me drive her car and borrow her clothes.

I also realized this wouldn't be a shopping extravaganza: Jenny only intended to buy one gift. I'd let envy take over my vision until it distorted the picture I had of my best friend. With that thought, the green-eyed monster seemed to shrink in size.

After we finished our cones, we headed for the next clothing store. "Look at that red sweater," Jenny said, as we passed the window. "It would be perfect for you, Teresa, with your dark hair. How are you doing saving your baby-sitting money? Soon maybe you'll have enough to buy something like that."

A few minutes ago, all I would have heard was the part about saving my baby-sitting money. I would have resented the fact that all Jenny had to do was ask her parents for the sweater, and they'd buy it for her. This time, though, I heard more. I heard my best friend complimenting me and saying how good I'd look. I heard the voice of someone who loved and cared for me for who I was. I needed to express the same to her.

"You know, Jen, I've been thinking," I said, linking arms with her and pulling her back to the first store, "that white skirt and sweater really was beautiful on you."

Teresa Cleary

"Brian just said he loves the way I dress.
Please promise you won't tell him
all the clothes I wear are yours."

As Close as Sisters

It was a balmy Virginia night when Shirley Bumgardner dropped in on Margaret Rowe to see if she was over her summer cold. Best friends for thirty years, they'd grown as close as sisters, so Shirley often came by.

She knocked on Margaret's door. No answer. "Probably just went to bed early," she shrugged. She turned to leave, but then something—a premonition, a touch of the coldest fear—stopped her in her tracks. She knocked harder. No answer. Slipping an emergency key from her pocket, she went inside.

"Oh, no!" Shirley gasped, when she saw Margaret sprawled across the bed, her face pale. "She looks like she's at death's door!"

Helping her friend into the car, Shirley whispered a prayer. "Please let someone be able to save my friend." Shirley never guessed that she herself might be that someone.

It had been a steamy afternoon in 1963 when Margaret stepped into the soothing coolness of the drugstore in Suffolk, Virginia, where Shirley worked as a pharmacist.

"Sometimes, I feel like I'm throwing good money after bad," Margaret sighed, handing over her prescription. "I take my medication but my blood pressure is still high."

"It'd be even higher if you didn't," cautioned Shirley. While she filled the order, the women, both in their thirties, chatted away.

"What a nice person," Shirley marveled, as Margaret left.

Then they began running into each other at the restaurants in Suffolk. Over lunches, they found they had a lot in common: an aversion to cooking, a love of travel, and the trials and tribulations of dating. Neither of them had found Mr. Right yet. "So in the meantime," they resolved, "we'll fill our lives with other things!"

Shirley bought the pharmacy, and Margaret grew to love her job as the office manager for an accounting firm. Margaret had family nearby, and both women made friends easily. They were in a bridge club that met regularly.

And they talked and talked—sharing gossip, secret worries and hopes.

"Best friends for life," they'd always say.

Then a few years ago, Margaret noticed she wasn't feeling as chipper as usual. "Probably just my blood pressure," she told herself. It had been high ever since she was a child. Though she took her medicine faithfully, she'd had tired spells before.

So she was shocked when she went in for a routine physical and her doctor told her, "I'm very sorry, but your kidneys are failing." A lifetime of high blood pressure, he said, had damaged them.

Stunned, Margaret stared at him.

"We can change my medication, right?" she asked.

"At this point," he said, his eyes soft with sympathy, "medication won't help."

"Then . . . isn't there *anything* you can do?" Margaret cried.

"You'll need a kidney transplant," he told her. "But with

so many on the list . . . your turn may not come up for a long time."

Margaret read between the lines all too well: *And I might not last that long.*

The office was quiet except for the ticking of the clock—and Margaret's muffled crying. "There's so much I still want to do!" she wept.

Driving home, Margaret's heart was heavy, but her mind was resolved. "I won't let this destroy the years I have left," she vowed.

In the morning, she mustered up enthusiasm and returned to work. And that night, though she told Shirley she was having kidney problems, she didn't let on just how serious her condition was.

But now, months later, as Shirley raced to the hospital, she realized just how sick her friend must be.

The next hours were agony. At the hospital, Shirley paced until the doctor appeared.

"How is she?" she cried.

"Not good, I'm afraid—she's in full kidney failure," he said. "She'll have to go on dialysis immediately."

Later that night, Shirley tried to hide her fear. "You'll be fine," she comforted Margaret.

Margaret smiled weakly. "Let's hope so."

For the next few months, Margaret underwent daily dialysis treatments. Yet despite them, she grew weaker. She knew that now, only a transplant would give her back her life. But doctors said the chances were that only a blood relative would be a match—and her brother couldn't donate because he'd had two heart attacks. "So does that mean Margaret will have to die waiting?" Shirley worried. "I can't let that happen!"

One afternoon, as the women sat talking, Margaret confided, "I'm so scared. What if they don't find a donor in time?"

Shirley paused. "I know the doctors will say there is little chance," she said. "But Margaret, I want to be tested. I want to donate my kidney."

"Shirley, I can't let you do that!" Margaret cried. "It's too risky."

Shirley gripped her hand. "We're best friends," she said. "If the shoe were on the other foot, you'd do it for me. Please let me try!"

Margaret's eyes shone with gratitude.

But the kidney specialist warned the women not to get their hopes up. Their blood and antigens would have to be compatible, she explained, something that usually happens only with siblings or parents and children. "The chances you'll be a match are a million to one—or worse," she cautioned.

Undeterred, Shirley and Margaret took the battery of tests—then waited . . .

Shirley was filling a prescription, when she picked up the phone to hear: "It's unbelievable, but you're a match!" the nurse said. "Surgery is a go!"

Shirley dropped the bottle, spilling pills all over the counter. "Thank you! Thank you!" she cried. Within weeks, the women checked into the hospital, nervous—but hopeful. "I'll always be grateful to you," Margaret told Shirley, as they waited in the hospital corridor. "You're the best friend I could ever have."

Six hours later, a voice pierced the fog in Shirley's brain. She opened her eyes.

"It was a success, dear," said a smiling nurse. "Your kidney is already working in your friend."

"We did it!" Shirley smiled—then drifted back to sleep.

A few weeks later, the friends were back home.

Now, months later, Shirley is fully recovered, and Margaret is getting stronger every day.

"I owe it all to Shirley," Margaret says. "She saved my life."

Shirley, meanwhile, is thumbing through travel brochures.

"We're going to Atlantic City as soon as Margaret is ready," she says, a mischievous light dancing in her eyes. "I figure that since we beat the odds once, we might get lucky again."

Heather Black

My Butterfly Friend

Carol and Fred were newcomers to our church. I wanted her to feel welcome, so I invited her to attend the monthly ladies' luncheon with me. She hesitated. "I have a rare heart disease that can only be treated with experimental medication. I never know when I'm feeling up to doing something. I'd really like to, but I'd better not plan on it. I'm sorry."

I was disappointed. I had immediately liked her and I wanted to get to know her better. She had such beautiful sparkling blue eyes and a smile that belied the fact that there was anything physically wrong with her.

As the months went by, we greeted each other in church, but every time an invitation was extended to do something, she refused. Still, Carol remained on my mind and in my heart, so I decided to try once more. This time, I invited her to attend a Bible study with me at another friend's home. "I don't even know if I could concentrate on the lesson. The heart medication slows everything down." Then, softly, she added, "I think I'd like to try."

As the weeks went by, Carol began to respond to the love shared at the study, and she participated more and more. Even when she wasn't feeling her best, she made the effort to attend, and we began to see a transformation. God was touching her heart, physically and spiritually.

One morning as we visited in the church foyer, my friend Darlene said, "Let's invite Carol to our pajama party!" This fun routine shared by Darlene and me had begun as a way to cure my loneliness when my husband was away on business trips. It seemed we never had enough time together, and there was always so much to talk and pray about. We invited Carol and were surprised and delighted when she said, "That sounds like fun! I'd love to come!"

She came through my door the next week with her arms loaded, then went back to the car to get her pajamas, pillow, comforter, teddy bear and everything else she needed to feel at home away from home. The three of us talked until the wee hours of the morning, and after a late breakfast, continued to talk on into the afternoon, still in our pajamas.

Many more pajama parties followed. Each time, the guest room Carol occupied became more and more like home, until she finally left her pillow, comforter and all the other things for the next time. Like a butterfly, she emerged from her cocoon.

Miraculously, more adventures began. We started going on little outings, then bigger and bigger ones. The highlight of our escapades was the three of us taking an overnight trip to attend *Oprah*. Eventually, trips to Disney World on her own were second nature to her.

But when her daughter called announcing Carol's impending grandmotherhood, some of Carol's old doubts resurfaced: "Can I be the kind of grandma I want to be? I want to have fun with my babies. I want to baby-sit for them, rock them, hold them and play with them." Carol's concerns about being physically able to care for her new grandson soon faded. The joy of holding him filled her heart to overflowing and her caregiving took over. And with the second grandchild, her heart's capacity and her ability doubled.

Last week she called, exclaiming, "I'm going to Europe! Five days in Paris and five days in Austria to celebrate Holly and Andy's anniversary. They want me to come to watch the grandkids while they enjoy evenings out. My doctor has given me permission to go! Can you believe it?"

I do believe it. Girlfriends and pajama parties are the best medicine.

Karen R. Kilby

7

FOREVER FRIENDS

We've been friends forever. I suppose that can't be true. There must have been a time before we became friends but I can't remember it. You are in my first memory and all my best memories ever since.

Linda MacFarlane

A Letter to Lois

Dear Lois,

I have been thinking a lot today about our friendship and all the things that made it so special. Although we had known each other since the seventh grade, it really started in the tenth grade. You would wait for me between second and third hour. I can still see you standing at the end of the hallway, with your arms full of books, so comfortable and confident. Remember Brandon Johnston? He used to wait with you sometimes. Even though he was older, he had a crush on you. Of course he did; they all had crushes on you! The florists made a fortune delivering yellow roses to your door.

I have often wondered what made you pick me. I was the opposite of you in every way. Not only in personality, but even in physical appearance. You were short, with dark hair and big, expressive brown eyes. Beautiful in ways that defied description. I was tall and blonde, with weird blue eyes. Beautiful is not an adjective I would have applied to myself. More than that, you were confident, strong-willed, stubborn and fifteen going on eighteen. I, on the other hand, was unsure, awkward and fifteen going on fifteen! I guess you took one look at me and decided you were my only hope.

We were also, as I recall, very different when it came to physical constitution. I would catch a cold, have a runny nose for a couple of days and maybe a cough. You would catch it from me and be ill for a week. One night after work, I got to your house, bouncing off the walls trying to decide what we were going to get into that night. There you were droopy-tailed and baggy-eyed, begging for a nap. I said, "Okay, one hour and then we're outta here!" We lay down and I immediately fell asleep. I woke exactly one hour later with you staring at me. "I hate you. You said I was the one who was tired, and YOU fell asleep!" You said you would hate to see what would cause me to lose sleep. As it turned out, the first night that I would lie awake was still nine years away. Although you would be the cause of that long and sleepless night, you weren't there to see it.

When I had my first child, I typically sailed through the pregnancy. Never once in nine months did I feel even the slightest tinge of nausea. I answered the phone one day when you were pregnant with Ryan to hear a voice that sounded like it was coming from the other side of hell saying, "How can anybody go through this and NEVER THROW UP?! I hang over the toilet all day, every day, cursing you. Whoever named this misery 'morning' sickness had to have been a man!" To which I replied, "I'm sorry." I had not been your friend all those years without learning when it was best to keep quiet. You were the only person I ever knew who had to be hospitalized for morning sickness.

To this day when I hear "Tin Man" by America, I can feel that great summer of 1974, between our junior and senior years, when we decided that fun was more important than money so we quit our jobs! Remember? We had great tans, little bitty blue jean cutoffs, halter tops, spoon rings and a '67 Mustang; everything we needed! Everything, that is, except money! I don't think one Whopper with pickle and onion on one side and ketchup on the other was what Burger King had in mind when they said, "Have it your way." We lived that summer on the kindness of others, and of our dates when we got really hungry. Sometimes, I play Eric Clapton's "I Shot the Sheriff" just to feel that six-teen-year-old rush again. It was the best of times to begin a friendship that would last a lifetime.

We had a lot of adventures and fun, times I wouldn't trade for anything in the world, but what I remember most are the feelings we shared. You were the one friend I could tell anything to. I could confess my meanest thoughts, my secret longings and most fragile feelings. I could show you all these sides of myself and know that you would still love me. I wasn't one of the prettiest or the most popular. I never wanted to be a cheerleader or go to the prom. I read strange books and used words most fifteen-year-olds had never heard. But you didn't care; you read the books and enjoyed the vocabulary as much as I did! We were probably the only teenage fans of *Reader's Digest: Improve Your Word Power.* I always knew the other girls wondered why you even bothered with me. I also knew, although you never said anything, that they gave you a hard time about it. But it was "Love me, love my dog" with you, so they accepted me because you did.

You taught me to have confidence. You believed in me and made me believe in myself. From the time we were fif-teen years old until we were grown with sons of our own, we were tell-your-deepest-feelings-to, laugh-until-you-cry, never-give-up-on-each-other best friends.

The day you married Chris, I called you from Germany, but it took so long for the call to get through it was time for you to leave for the church. But you wouldn't leave until you talked to me. Once we started talking, we didn't want to say good-bye, so you were almost late for your own wedding. That became a pattern with us: never wanting to say good-bye.

I still have the sand castle you gave me the night you left for Texas. We went to Darryl's for dinner and had such a great time. All night, we avoided talking about the reason we were together. It was there, though, sitting at the table like an ugly, unwelcome guest. Later, as we stood in the street outside my house, the time finally came to say good-bye. Then the tears came, and we cried and laughed at the same time. We planned the next time we would see each other; that way we could just say "see ya later," instead of "good-bye." We were never very good at saying good-bye. The card you gave me that night with the castle said we were: "Forever friends, and forever friends were never apart."

It seemed no matter where we lived, when we called or saw each other, everything was the same. The world changed and our lives took us in different directions, but our friendship was constant. I knew I could always count on you.

There was one time, in particular, when life was really getting me down; I felt as if I were suffocating. You lived in Dallas, Ryan had just been born and I called you one Monday to see what you were doing on Thursday. You said nothing, so I asked if you would mind picking me up at the airport. I didn't need the phone company's assistance to hear your answer. Those four days were some of the best of my life. I don't think we stopped talking from the time you picked me up until you took me back to the airport on Sunday. You even slept on the couch bed with me. I have the picture Chris took of us at two in the morning, still up and talking. It is framed and sits on my bedroom shelf beside the memory box you made me. I find it ironic that you made me a memory "box." A box could never contain all my memories of the times I have with you. Nothing could ever contain my memories: They burst the seams of my heart and flood my soul with the bittersweet feelings of growing up, and innocence lost.

It's funny, you always think you will see it coming, like in the movies. There will be some mysterious, inexplicable feeling, an ominous premonition, some kind of sign. But life doesn't work that way; it just hits you when you aren't looking. In a heartbeat, your life can change forever.

The call came at about ten that awful night. Your sister called to tell me you had been in a terrible accident. They only gave you a 50 percent chance of survival. When I hung up, I knew you would make it; there was never a second that I thought otherwise. I was making plans to come to Dallas to help you recover. While I was planning my trip, the telephone rang again. "They couldn't save her; she's gone," is all I remember your sister saying. Then I was on the kitchen floor, my arms wrapped around my knees, slowing rocking back and forth. How could you be gone? I didn't get to tell you good-bye. That night I saw every hour strike on the bedside clock; I never closed my eyes. It was the first time I ever lay awake all night.

Two days later, Chris brought you home. I was so scared to walk into that room. I didn't make it the first time. I ran away and stood looking blindly out the window, fists balled tightly in my pockets and silently pleading to wake up from this horrible dream, to be allowed to escape what I knew I was about to see. Standing there at the window, tears streaming down my face, I realized I was looking at the tire dealer across the street, where we had stolen a tire one night to play a practical joke during that magical summer of '74. I felt your presence at my side as surely as if you were standing there. Desperately clinging to the memory of those two young girls, hearing their laughter, I turned and walked to where you lay. Looking down at you, I felt my heart and soul shatter, never to be completely whole again. Later, I placed a single yellow rose in your hands so you would always have something you loved, something from me. The hardest part of all was to come the next day, when I had to walk away and leave you at the cemetery. I tried, but as I turned to walk away, I had the horrible, crushing realization that if I walked away, the past few days were real. I was never again going to laugh with you, cry with you or share my life with you. When I walked away, you would be gone from me forever.

It has been fourteen years this month since that day. I have had two more sons of my own, and I have watched your son grow into a fine young man; you would be very proud of him. Every time I look into his beautiful, dark eyes, I see you looking back. He has your mark on him—there is no doubt—and your hand will be forever on his heart. I have lost my grandmother, my father and my mother. I've been through a divorce and remarried. Not one single day has passed that I don't think of you and wish you were here. I still take yellow roses to your grave, and I haven't missed giving your mother a card on Mother's Day in thirteen years. Last year, I left a card and a rose on the front porch for her to find. I thought you would like that.

Sometimes, I wonder what our conversations would be like now. I suppose we would be a little wiser and a bit more mature. I am sure you would still be the beautiful, self-confident one helping me to find my way. The one thing I know without a moment's hesitation is we would still be the tell-your-deepest-feelings-to, laugh-until-you-cry, never-give-up-on-each-other best friends we were from fifteen to twenty-six. I also knew without a doubt that I am a better person for having known you.

I miss you, Lois, as much today as I did fourteen years ago. There is an aching emptiness in my heart that will never ease. I love you; I will always love you.

I guess I still haven't learned how to say good-bye. I doubt I ever will.

Beth Sherrow

A Friend for All Seasons

The growth of true friendship maybe a lifelong affair.

Sarah Orne Jewett

Some friends in your life come and go, and some come and stay. And when it comes time to let them go, though painful, it feels right and brings peace. For you know that you have given and received unconditional love and acceptance, with no regrets. That was how it was with my friend Sue.

As a nurse at a local hospital, I facilitated the discharge planning conferences. Sue, an animated redhead and a dietitian on the oncology floors, always attended these meetings. She loved her patients and had a reputation for going the extra mile to be sure each one got the special nutrients needed to fight the cancer. We bonded instantly, beginning a twenty-year friendship that would take us on many twists and turns as we journeyed through life together.

"You know, we must somehow be sisters. Both our

moms are elementary teachers and pack rats," Sue laughed early on in our friendship.

Before long, people told us we started to look alike. Some thought we were really sisters.

We shared the good times and celebrated each passing year. Sue had a zest for life. I could count on her to welcome each season and holiday in an appropriate outfit with matching earrings that made us all smile. Nothing in my life was trivial to her. When it came time for me to marry at age thirty-six, I wanted an outdoor wedding but feared rain. "Why not have it at our house? We can decorate the garden and move to our church down the road if it rains," she offered. So my husband and I married at her beautiful colonial home in the country, where Sue catered the reception herself. From the rehearsal dinner to our wedding night in her comfortable master suite before departing on our honeymoon, Sue made this occasion a time to remember. Six years later, she opened her home once again for a dinner that celebrated the baptism of our only daughter.

But life has it highs and lows, and so did our friendship.

"I think I may have to put Poopsie down," she cried after her beloved mutt was hit by a car on the road to her house.

I rushed with her to the vet. Poopsie miraculously survived but lost bowel and bladder control; the vet gave no guarantee for recovery. My nursing came in handy as I taught Sue how to catheterize her pup until function returned.

Then, my sixteen-year-old cat, Grace, had to be put to sleep. I grieved and sought Sue's comfort, freely given.

But nothing prepared us for the next tragic discovery.

Sue started seeing shooting lights inside her eyes. An exam revealed a rare form of ocular cancer; her prognosis was ten years, at best. After surgery, I assisted by putting eyedrops in her eyes and cheering her on. "Please take some antioxidants, Susie," I begged. "Your immune system has got to stay strong to beat this."

With a smile, she would always say, "You know I believe you can get all you need through eating a balanced diet."

This optimistic dietitian refused to heed my pleas.

Soon afterward, it was my turn: I discovered a mass in my breast. Although I walked alone into the cold office for the defining ultrasound test, Sue suddenly appeared with an angel penny bookmark for me. "I did not want you to be here by yourself," she whispered, as she hugged me and joined me for the wait. Weeks later, she would again show up at the hospital outpatient surgery suite, with flowers and a big smile. She never forgot to be there for me.

"Sue's mother has been killed in a car wreck," I heard the voice on the phone say. It seemed unreal, as I had shared dinner with her mom a few days prior. In a freakish accident, she had been hit by an eighteen-wheeler. Sue and I held hands as we confirmed her mom's identity at the county morgue. Sue took an extended family leave but never seemed to heal completely after this loss. Her exuberance for life dimmed as she faced a future without her best supporter.

Sue loved taking pictures and became an amateur photographer. Each year brought more memories, recorded in photographs, confirming our blessings. My husband gave me a surprise fiftieth birthday party, and Sue was on board with her camera.

Two weeks later, she showed up with a photo album and bad news: a recurrence of her cancer was confirmed. It had been eleven years since her first diagnosis. Her abdomen was swollen, with liver metastasis the suspected cause. She felt bad all the time but kept wearing her bright-colored pantsuits with the elastic waistbands.

One Monday, Sue called to ask if I could take her to the

hospital. Immediately, I drove to her home. We walked through her yard for a while, discussing all the times we had shared there. Finally she said, "I am ready now. I think this may be the last time." Sue had become a registered nurse a few years prior and worked with hospice. Trusting her judgment, I feared the worst. That long drive was the last one. Despite the best efforts of excellent physicians and state-of-the-art treatments, Sue's condition worsened. Only a few weeks later, I sat at her bedside as she slipped in and out of consciousness. We had a brief but meaningful visit, during which she recognized me. As I held her hand, she told me she loved me. I whispered that it was time for her to go see her mom, and that I would be there soon as well. Because we were Christians, we knew we would meet again in a place with no sickness or pain.

Just two days before Christmas, heaven had a new angel—and my life would never be the same.

Marylane Wade Koch

Lucky Charms

Katie and I met on the first day of graduate school. We were paired to share an apartment, and became inseparable almost immediately. An unlikely pair at first glance—a short, tanned California surfer girl and a tall, pale Scandinavian ice queen—we had more in common than we initially expected. Katie was the youngest of our class, and I, an only child, had always yearned for a sibling. I quickly became Katie's surrogate older sister, whom she missed terribly, and I finally found the little sister I never had.

Our friendship was permanently sealed that particular night when I was awakened by the creaking of my bedroom floor. The streetlight illuminated my room around the edges of the blinds, and I could make out Katie standing by my bed, in her little-girl nightie, sobbing uncontrollably.

"What's wrong, Katie?" I shrieked, expecting the worst.

"I had a bad dream," she sobbed. "Can I cuddle up with you?"

Dumbfounded, I lifted up the covers and made room for her next to me. She crawled in, and I, somewhat hesitantly, started to pat her back and stroke her hair until her sobbing seemed to calm and finally stop. Eventually her rhythmic breathing suggested that she had fallen asleep. I, still wide awake, suddenly realized how comforting it was to have her in my life.

Although, after graduation, our lives took us separate ways—initially to different coasts, and later to different countries and even continents—we were adamant about making our friendship work across time zones. Because we both were die-hard travelers, we easily fell into the pattern of meeting each other at exotic places around the world— and getting ourselves into all sorts of mischief along the way. Whether we were bullying each other into bungee jumping in New Zealand, getting our SUV stuck in the sand and subsequently being chased by baboons in Kenya, experiencing an earthquake in the Cascades or praying for our lives while riding a tiny Italian sports car through serpentine roads in the Italian Alps—somehow, we always managed to emerge safe and in good spirits. Nothing ever fazed us because we truly believed that we were invincible when we were around each other—we were each other's lucky charm. Although we both had our share of disasters and difficulties over the years, just a visit from our lucky charm was usually sufficient to change any situation for the better.

A few years ago I was Katie's maid of honor at her last-minute wedding to her longtime boyfriend. In true Katie style she told me upon my arrival that I was responsible for her hair and makeup because she could not find a professional to do it for her on such short notice. I almost fainted but she winked at me.

"Come on, girlfriend! We survived so many trials and tribulations together. You are not going to bail on me on this one, are you? You never complained about any-thing—not even when I forgot to pick you up in Lisbon, or when I got us lost in Morocco or even when I bailed on you with the term paper. So why are you so afraid to blow-dry my hair and to help me put on a little mascara?"

She was right. This was Katie, after all—who never took

life too seriously and never conformed to rules unless she was entirely sure what purpose they were meant to serve.

As I walked down the aisle behind her we were captured on my favorite snapshot—Katie looking back at me. Light on make-up and heavy on natural beauty, with her long, blonde hair loosely framing her exquisite features and radiant smile. During our last get-together, a relatively subdued stopover in New York City, she excitedly told me that she and her husband had started trying for a baby. I, still single and electrified by the prospect of becoming an "aunt," did not realize until my flight back home that this might actually be the end of our carefree existence and of the main chapter of our friendship.

Although still very happy for my dear friend, I suddenly felt lonely and ancient. The memories of our trips and our laughter came flowing back to me, and I couldn't refrain from crying. I was angry with myself for feeling this way. "Change is good," I told myself, and "we need to move on with our lives. We need to cherish the past and look forward to the future." I forced myself to think of happy memories and made a fool of myself for the rest of the flight as I periodically laughed out loud over our funniest escapades. I decided not to share my worries with Katie, and over the next few days I started feeling better about it—although I still got teary eyed from time to time.

Then one morning, I had an e-mail from Katie waiting in my inbox. Not knowing what news to expect, I clicked on it anxiously and read the three short but quite familiar sentences: "One-week beginners' windsurfing trip to the Dominican Republic. In two weeks. Are you game or lame?"

Damn. Did I just waste several days worrying about how our friendship might transform? How stupid of me to think that my lucky charm would, or could, ever change. We will be grandmothers and she will still bully me into climbing Mount Whitney, not stopping until she has chased me all the way up the mountain.

Monika Szamko

Minnie Pauz

And they wonder why women
go to the restroom in pairs!

Love Beyond Tears

Some people come into our lives and quickly go. Some people stay for a while and leave their footprints on our hearts, and we are never, ever the same.

Flavia

Julie was five years old when we first met in 1967. "This is Julie. She's my friend." My daughter, Susan, introduced us one morning after kindergarten.

The girls became fast friends. They were inseparable, singing silly songs as they squeezed into one overstuffed living room chair laughing until tears streamed down their faces.

Julie's mom and I took turns transporting the toothless and giggly twosome back and forth from our home to theirs. But the trips ended when my Susan was stricken with a brain tumor in 1969 at the age of seven.

During Susan's twenty-one month illness, Julie never stopped visiting. The girls played finger games when Susan's eyesight dimmed. Julie flipped phonograph records and kept right on singing with Susan, never asking why Susan no longer raced through the house, spun the hula hoop, attended ballet classes or ice-skated. Whenever Susan phoned to invite her friend for dinner, Julie jubilantly arrived to share a meal at Susan's bedside.

In June 1971, Susan died. Julie visited a few weeks later to spend time with our family, but her best friend was gone. Seeing the sadness in Julie's eyes, I told her that Susan loved Jesus and was probably singing with the angels in heaven.

Julie continued to drop by occasionally. On my first Mother's Day following Susan's death, Julie popped in with a red rose. A tradition was started that Sunday in 1972. Julie has never missed giving me a rose and special card on Mother's Day.

That isn't all. Throughout her school years, Julie invited me and my husband, Phil, to important class activities. At graduation, I watched her receive her diploma and knew Susan was there in spirit with her classmates. And when Julie, a member of the yearbook staff, handed me the 1980 yearbook, I opened it to find a dedication to Susan.

Before long, Julie was engaged and planning her wedding to Rob. I was not forgotten. At her shower, Julie's sister, Allison, quietly whispered, "If Susan were here, she'd be up front with Julie."

Another surprise awaited me on Julie and Rob's wedding day. I responded to Julie's telephone request to come to her home. She was waiting for me with a photographer. As she pinned a corsage on my dress and the camera clicked, she invited Phil and me to sit behind her parents in church.

And when Julie and Rob bought their home in Gardner, Massachusetts, of course, we were invited over.

Julie and I have become good friends. Our paths cross, part and unite again. Although we both lead busy lives, when we get together, it's like we never missed a moment. We meet for lunch and enjoy catching up on each other's lives. Julie asks about Phil, our son, Michael, and daughter, Kristin, their spouses and our delightful grandchildren. I listen as she fills me in on her mom and dad, her two sisters, Allison and Tammy, and their families.

Julie, like the five-year-old I first met, can still enthusiastically bring happiness into a dull day. She never fails to mention Susan and the meaning of their deep friendship at such a young age. She remarked, "I never knew Susan was that sick."

I asked why she continued to visit. "After all, you were only nine when Susan died."

"I felt like I belonged in your house. I was always there with Susan. My mother never told me to come; it was what I wanted to do."

Julie isn't afraid to say, "I know whenever I'm going through a hard time, Susan is up there for me."

Julie continues to enrich my life. Over the telephone, I learned of her pregnancy. "If it's a girl, I'd like to use the name Susan for her middle name," Julie announced.

This time, I burst into tears. How did Julie know I secretly prayed for Susan's name to be carried on?

Carley Susan Walsh was born October 10, 1997. When I cuddled her in my arms, I felt such love.

For seven years now, I've enjoyed all the hugs and kisses just like my other grandchildren. To Carley I am Granny Phyllis. I'm always invited to her ballet recitals, birthday parties and all the highlights in her life. Julie's joyful, gentle, loving spirit and compassionate heart never stop touching my life.

Today, I remember two five-year-old girls, Susan and Julie, whose paths crossed, then divided, but in truth, never really separated. Through their lives, God has taught me lessons I might never have understood otherwise.

I believe God, in his ultimate plan, brought Julie into my life to walk beside me, to share, care and remind me that God never leaves us comfortless.

Phyllis Cochran

Letters in Cement

A friendship can weather most things and thrive in thin soil—but it needs a little mulch of letters and phone calls and small silly presents every so often—just to save it from drying out completely.

Pam Brown

Digging deep into my hope chest, through the layers of my life, I find a lumpy fabric bag tied closed with string. I hesitate before opening it—getting into this veritable Pandora's box could take all day. Inside this ordinary looking bag are no fewer than thirty handwritten memories, wacky correspondence thick in their letter-size envelopes, colored with felt marker, stuck with snazzy stickers, postage stamped and sent halfway around the world. An entire year of one person's life. And not just any person, but my best friend.

Looking back now with the wisdom that ten years post–high school provides, I clearly see that my friends, my true friends, those who supported me during those formative teenage years, knew me better at the time than anyone else could have. Essentially, my friends were a part of my family, the people I saw every day at school, and the ones who saw me at my best and at my worst. It wasn't my parents who had a handle on where I was in life—it was my friends. Well, actually, one friend in particular: Lianne.

Lianne and I met the first day of seventh grade. We were the shortest two in the class. The similarities ended there—she loved cats, I had dogs; she was dark haired, I was blonde; she went away to camp every summer, I stayed home and joined 4-H; she was popular, I was awkward and goofy. We were always comfortably ourselves with each other, something that laid a lasting foundation for the wonderful, sometimes convoluted, journey ahead.

Fast-forward to tenth grade. I took my cues from Lianne as to what to wear, how to act around boys, what was cool. Lianne always had an easy time of making new friends. Awkward and shy, I did not. High school intimidated me, and my self-esteem suffered.

One chilly November morning, Lianne swallowed a whole bunch of Tylenol. I couldn't understand why. I was angry but at the same time relieved that she hadn't come to me with her problem. I was a naive fourteen; I wouldn't have known what to do. She recovered completely, the whole ordeal making her more accessible to me, more human. I saw her less as the "popular one," and more as another confused teenager, just as I was. From that point on, we were exclusive best friends.

There are your parents' rules—don't drink, don't smoke, home by midnight. And then there are the real life lessons your friends teach you—what it feels like to be kissed by a boy, how to smoke a cigarette, how to laugh your head off for hours at a time. Both provide equally valuable life lessons. Lianne taught me to not take myself too seriously.

She could make me crack up with just one look, just one quip.

To say I loved her like a sister would be wrong—I have a sister—it wasn't that way at all. Yet I loved her more strongly than that generic term "friend." She was almost a part of me: a limb, or an organ. When she left for a yearlong student exchange to New Zealand at the end of twelfth grade, it felt like someone had lopped off a very important part of me and sent it away with her.

I was happy for her—what a great opportunity to see the world, to get away from whatever it was at home that made her try to kill herself a few years earlier. Selfishly, I was absolutely miserable. I was lost without her. I wrote my first letter to her before she'd even flown across the Pacific Ocean. Being so accustomed to sharing every last detail of our lives with each other, a thick letter arrived every other week, the envelopes decorated with stickers and markers. We had a pretty good schedule—a letter from me to her one week, and one back the following week, and so on. Nothing at home could be as exciting as the life she was leading so far away—sailing, mountain climbing, vacationing with her host family, parties with her new friends. Celebrating her eighteenth birthday. Freedom.

Things hadn't been the same for me since she'd left—I was reeling from the gap left by Lianne's departure, and any support system I had was two weeks away by mail. I just didn't trust anyone besides her, couldn't ask anyone else what to do, couldn't talk to anyone else like I could talk to her. New friendships felt artificial. Yet, I finished high school while she was away and started university. I began dating and fell in love with the man I would later marry. I did it all on my own, proving to myself that I was strong enough to live, strong enough to be independent, strong enough to figure it all out by myself. I had grown up.

I had made a new life for myself during the year Lianne was gone, forged a very important relationship, taken some giant steps away from the girl I was and toward the woman I hoped to become. It took what seemed like forever, but the gap that she had left behind had closed before I'd even realized.

One day, after keeping the date of her return a secret, Lianne appeared at my door. We spent the next few days and nights together. While I had missed her very much, I felt completely monopolized by her. The love of my life was wondering why I had suddenly disappeared. Finally, after one drunken night, Lianne fell apart. Lying on a cot in her new room, in her new house (sadly, her parents had separated while she was gone), I could hear her sobbing down the hall. Things were really not the same—I knew it and I think she did, too, but our friendship was all that was familiar to her, all that was certain, and I had failed her.

Ironically, it wasn't until after Lianne returned home that our lives became officially separate. We drifted, hardly speaking to each other throughout the space of a year or two. Then one day, moving into our new house, I came across her letters while I was cleaning up. I went to throw them out and then hesitated. I started reading and realized that these had become as much her journal to me as my letters had been to her. I thought about sending them to her as a record of her time away, but the strings of my heart tugged me away from that idea. I thought she probably wouldn't want them and I would hate for her to toss them—so many hours of writing, so much thought put into them, not to mention the entertainment value of marker-scrawled inside jokes written from one seventeen-year-old girl to another, the hilarity of our simplistic view of the world. No, I would need to hold on to these for myself.

The electronic age facilitated my "reunion" with Lianne. I ran into her by chance one night and got her e-mail address. We rekindled our friendship in much the same fashion as we had kept it going when she was halfway around the world: through correspondence. Our e-mail is riddled with, "Do you remember when . . ." and "Can you believe that. . . ." Gone are the markers and stickers, gone are the gaudy envelopes, but in their place is mail that still makes me smile, still touches me, still makes me try to restrain my out-loud laughing at the office. Still my best friend, my soul sister.

I got an e-mail from Lianne a few weeks ago. She informed me that she had found a box with the letters I had sent to her in New Zealand. She had packed it years ago, numbering every single letter. She said that some were sad, but they were mostly funny and that we should get together and read them; maybe it was crazy, but she'd kept every single one of them. One whole year of my life.

Now at very different stages in our lives, Lianne and I live four hours apart and try to get together whenever she's home. Maybe it wasn't healthy to be such exclusive best friends as we were, especially being only seventeen, but there are only certain people who can make you laugh hysterically, and only special ones who are privy to your innermost thoughts, and only the privileged few who have seen you cry. Lianne was the best friend who prepared me for life, the one who set the bar so high for my next best friend and soul mate: my husband.

Indeed, though we may travel in and out of some lives but once, there are others through which we tread constantly, even if we're not always around. Lianne certainly weaves her way through my life every day because I carry her, and the spirit of who I was when I was around her, in my heart always. In the grand scheme of life, those years from junior high until the end of high school are very short. However fleeting they are, it is the decisions then and the people we choose to interact with that lay the foundation for who we will be for the rest of our lives.

To say that Lianne is but one brick in that foundation would be modest. I would say that one day we rented a cement mixer, went shopping for some cute outfits to wear, guessed how much sand and water to pour in, and turned out two pretty snazzy foundations upon which we continue to build our lives. Oh yeah, and we each cast our handprints into the other's wet cement.

Jennifer Nicholson

The Face of Hope

The first time I met Marlene, more than three decades ago, our family had just moved to a small valley rich in fishing, a wilderness populated by Norwegians and The Nuxalk Native Tribe. Marlene's mother had been a mail-order bride from Germany, and they had moved to the valley a few years before.

Marlene was the prettiest girl I'd ever seen. She had pale blonde hair and shy, sky-blue eyes. We were in the fourth grade when we met, and she sat beside me in class. Because our families were regarded as outsiders, not being Native or Norwegian, Marlene and I developed an instant camaraderie. We shared everything; everything in our hearts and in our minds, our secrets, our desires and our dreams.

We both married young, still teens. She married a Nuxalk Native Indian whose father was a famous grizzly bear guide. I married a Frenchman from the city. We both had daughters.

In time, Marlene and I both divorced. I moved out of the valley for several years, while Marlene stayed on in her little house by the river, a beautiful white woman living with the tribe her daughter, Phoebe, was born into.

When I moved back to the valley with my daughter, and Marlene and I hooked up again, becoming as inseparable as ever. We were like sisters, always there for one another, and, like sisters, we had our occasional squabbles, misunderstandings and jealousies, like when one snapped up the boyfriend the other one wanted. But we always made up.

Our daughters grew up to be friends, too, and spent many weekends together sharing their lives, the way Marlene and I shared ours.

When we finally went our separate ways, living in separate cities, we lost contact with each other. For a time it seemed the cord of friendship had weakened between us, but in reality, it just became buried under the load single working mothers face.

My daughter went on to college, and Marlene's daughter dabbled in photography. I encouraged her to go into modeling because she was so stunning, just like her mother. But Phoebe was shy and sweet, and had the Native's love for solitude and forests, and so declined the modeling offers that came her way.

I loved that girl like a second daughter, and as with my own daughter I encouraged her to follow her dreams. But her dreams proved to be short-lived.

A cold, dark chill gripped my insides as I stared into the California sunshine, with the smell of frying chicken cozily wafting through my small kitchen. My week-old wedding photo was still on the refrigerator, and my eyes wandered to it as I tried to assimilate the gross hideous thing coiling through the telephone wire. "It's true," my mother told me long-distance, "Phoebe is dead."

Denial rang through me as my mother gave a sketchy outline of the murder the night before. I could almost taste Marlene's despair as if it were my own, and I said a prayer for strength and wisdom as I dialed her number. Her wailing pierced my heart, as we clung in spirit to one another across thousands of miles. With a bereaved rage, I knew that two murders had been committed, not one. The bodily destruction of Phoebe, and the spiritual destruction of Marlene, her mother. My best friend.

"I'll be there. Tomorrow." I wept as the image of Phoebe filled my mind. Phoebe. Spectacularly beautiful, spectacularly sweet. I shut my eyes in a spasm of pain as I thought of my own daughter. How was it possible for my friend to bear such a monumental agony as this?

Marlene hung up the phone, and I went to tell my new husband that I was going to Canada the following day.

When I got off the plane in Vancouver, my sister and I drove to Marlene's house on the island.

We were immediately enveloped by the scent of hundreds of flowers and the warm arms of Marlene and her sisters, as we all wept. This was a pain nobody was prepared for.

The day before the funeral, I went downstairs to Marlene's office and with the gorgeous face of Phoebe before me—her photograph alive with joy and vibrant expectation—I wrote her eulogy.

The next day, Marlene and I clasped hands tightly as the funeral car bore us inexorably to the place of good-bye. Somehow, God gave me the strength to deliver the eulogy. I looked at my friend with sympathy that words could not convey. But too short was the saying of hello and good-bye to the life of someone so rare and sweet, someone who should never have left the Earth in such a violent way.

I stayed behind in the chapel after the service. So I was there to see Marlene, sobbing brokenly, throw herself upon her daughter's coffin and beg her not to leave. That sheer grief, so stark and powerful and shattering, as Marlene clung to the coffin of Phoebe, weeping inconsolably, with her husband clinging to her, snapped the thin threads holding my own heart together. I thought of my only daughter, and the idea of losing her through strangulation at the hands of her estranged boyfriend, as Marlene had lost Phoebe, was too much to bear.

It took a long time for Marlene's husband to pry her away from her only child whom she did not have the strength of mind or will to part with. But somehow, between us, we managed to get her home.

A few days later, Marlene and I pulled out three decades of photographs from her shelves. As we sat on the floor of her recreation room, we laughed and cried for hours over the years of our lives and the lives of our children, the pictures of youth and hope and strength. And the bond between us forged into steel.

There is a huge collage of Phoebe that Marlene put together shortly after her death. It chronicles her life and hangs on the wall of Marlene's living room. On the mantel, an urn with Phoebe's ashes, the badge of a mother's pain, sits in the place of honor.

It is now two years after Phoebe's death. Marlene still has a great task ahead of her. But it is a noble task that will enable her to keep putting one foot in front of the other, to keep going on, a task that has the power to rebuild her soul.

I have looked into the face of that task. It is the face of trust.

Phoebe's son, Dylan, four years old now, his face sparkling with the shy smile of the mother he lost, the mother he told me was dancing with the angels, is the face of the future. The face of love. The face of Marlene's greatest treasure. And the face of her hope.

Janet Hall Wigler

The Artist's Chair

Friendship is one of the sweetest joys of life.
Many might have failed beneath the bitterness of
their trial had they not found a friend.

Charles H. Spurgeon

It looked just like an old chair discarded by the roadside along with the week's trash. My dear friend and sister-in-law, Sue, who is an artist, announced, "That's an antique. I've seen that chair in famous paintings. It's an artist's chair."

And so we struggled, carrying it the six blocks toward home, each of us taking a side and holding on dearly. Finally, the white wooden chair with the slats in its back and the graceful circular arms was placed on my porch. Once removed from the trash that had surrounded it, the chair assumed a regal pose, as if it were meant to seat a king or queen. One could easily envision an artist like Sue capturing its majesty on canvas. I knew that was her intention.

We thought Sue would take the chair back with her to

Maryland, four hours away, but the chair had other ideas. It would not fit in the backseat of the car. No matter how we tried, pushing and prodding, it refused to cooperate. The trunk, filled with suitcases from a family of four, was not an option. And neither was tying it to the top of the new car. "I guess I'll have to leave it here until next time," Sue muttered, casting a loving glance in its direction.

I waved good-bye and comfortably settled down in the artist's chair. The next time, we faced the same car, the same problems. Too many suitcases, too many people. There was something about the way the arms curved that caused it to protrude in impossible directions. "We'll take it another time," Sue vowed. Again and again, we tried. Even with fewer suitcases or fewer travelers, the chair remained stubborn—always inches from our goal. It was as if it was determined to remain on my porch.

I had no objection to its decision. I had grown accustomed to doing my afternoon daydreaming there, and each day I looked forward to its delicate beauty. Of course, it didn't hurt that it was the only chair noticed by anyone who walked onto my porch.

It remained there for one year, then two. Summer storms beat down upon it, and winter covered it with ice and heavy snow. The white artist's chair withstood the harsh weather with a majesty unequaled by any other chair on the porch.

At the end of the second summer, I put an extra coat of white paint on my chair. That's the way I thought of it now. So when Sue mused one day, "I wonder if I'll ever get that chair to Maryland," I thought it time to set the matter straight. Though I offered the words mixed with laughter, she could not mistake their meaning when I added, "You had your chance. It's become my chair now. I just couldn't part with it. It's a member of my family."

We did not speak of it further. I moved the chair inside the house in the third year. It remained in my living room, and later I moved it upstairs to the guest room, where I did my serious thinking. I placed a flowered pillow in its crevice, a plant to the right of it and a white pitcher to the left.

I convinced myself that it was content and safe and that it knew it had found a secure home. The room was sun filled and occasionally one cat or the other would curl on the pillow and fill the chair with purring. As the fifth year wore on, and I had every right to feel the chair was mine (for Sue never mentioned it again), I often noticed her long thoughtful glances whenever she looked in its direction. I assured myself it wasn't my fault. The artist's chair was where it chose to be.

Years later, when the chair had become a fixture in our home and I no longer thought of it as special, when all thoughts of an artist capturing its spirit had faded, Sue experienced a difficult time with the flu and viruses that hit her one after the other. She wasn't at work in her art studio, and she didn't want to talk about it, even to me. I, in turn, was frustrated with my work, unable to fasten on any long-term writing goals. I didn't want to talk about that, either. Our deep relationship had been built on the writer and artist supporting each other. Our conversations grew shorter. The list of things we wouldn't talk about grew longer.

One weekend, Sue's children visited without their parents. All during their stay, I thought of my dear friend who had remained at home. I missed her and needed her friendship and realized I was letting it slip through my fingers.

I sat down on the artist's chair to think about it, to think about the years that Sue and I had enjoyed supporting one another, always giving more, as if we had an endless supply of sharing. From where I sat, I could see the car my niece and nephew had driven to my house. It was a new car, a larger one. *Forget it,* I told myself. *You can think of something else beside the chair to make Sue understand how you feel about her.*

I drove to the bakery and bought half a dozen chocolate cupcakes (Sue's favorite), four bran muffins and two dozen hard rolls. I took out the two vases I had discovered at a garage sale. I was saving them for her next visit. Often I would find pottery she could capture in her still-life paintings. I wrapped all the gifts carefully and placed them in the trunk of the car. But inside, deep inside where the truth often hides, I knew what I had to do and what I had to give.

"Remember," I told my nephew, David, as he carried the artist's chair down the long stairway. "If this doesn't go in the backseat of the car easily, we don't push, we don't shove, we don't force it."

But I knew it would. Easily, gently, as if it were ready to say good-bye, to travel where it knew it belonged.

That night Sue called, her energy and excitement bursting through the telephone. "I can't believe you gave me the chair," she kept repeating. "I know how you love it. I promise I'll take good care of it and love it just as much." And then we talked about all the things we weren't able to talk about before.

The chair is in Sue's art studio in Maryland, and I shall probably never find another like it. But then again, I'll never be able to duplicate the friendship I share with Sue.

Harriet May Savitz

[AUTHOR'S NOTE: *The painting* The Artist's Chair, *by my friend Susan Blatstein, has been in exhibits at The Woodmere Museum in Chestnut Hill, Pennsylvania, and at The Government House, Annapolis, Maryland. Susan Blatstein passed away in April 2000.*]

Cece and Agnes

Constant use had not worn ragged the fabric of their friendship.

Dorothy Parker

Cecelia and Agnes did not become good friends until many years after they first met. Cecelia was nearly ten years older than Agnes, so they did not know each other, despite living in the same rural community. Their relationship began as in-laws, brought together when Cecelia's daughter married Agnes's son. Later, after both women's husbands died, they became closer than ever, conversing several times each week and often traveling together.

In the early years of their friendship, Cecelia and Agnes saw each other mainly at family gatherings. They loved attending the various celebratory events of their children's lives. Birthdays, anniversaries and the holidays were times of shared happiness. After the deaths of their husbands, Agnes and Cecelia consoled each other in their grief and eventually became the best of friends. They watched with pride as their children became grand-parents, and every new addition to their families brought them more joy. As their families became more indepen-dent, Cecelia and Agnes ventured beyond their small Midwestern hometown to explore the United States together.

After many years of enjoying each other's company, the years finally took their toll on Cecelia. As the older woman approached her mid-eighties, her mind became more and more confused. Cecelia's family eventually had to make the difficult decision to move her to a nursing home. Agnes, on the other hand, remained busy as ever, her mind sharp and her wit quick.

A true friend, Agnes was determined to help Cecelia in whatever way she could, especially on her almost daily visits to her friend in the nursing home. For several years beyond the time when Cecelia could recognize her, Agnes kept coming to see and talk to "Cece." As Agnes approached her eighties, she wondered why Cece contin-ued to live, it seemed, long past her prime. She com-mented frequently to the nurses at the home, "God must have forgotten my friend Cece. If I go first, I will tell him to go and get her, and bring her straight to heaven!" Everyone laughed, never dreaming that Agnes—the pic-ture of health herself—would go first.

But Agnes did die first, one frigid December morning, without any warning to her many friends and family members. The family was devastated by this unexpected shock. Agnes's funeral was delayed for several days; it was so cold, the ground was frozen solid.

Finally, the family was able to gather to celebrate Agnes's life. As her son and daughter-in-law prepared to leave for the church, they received a call from the nursing home informing them that their children's other grand-mother, Cecelia, had just passed away.

As the news of Cecelia's death spread throughout the church during Agnes's funeral, one might have been surprised to see smiles and hear a few chuckles at such a sad event. Yet those who knew the two women well, and had heard Agnes's promise to "talk to God" if she got to heaven first, were immediately consoled in their grief. The two best friends were together again at last, joined with their creator and each other forever.

Mary Treacy O'Keefe

More Than Ever

We had not seen each other for thirty years. Neither of us knew how that had happened. We had been dear friends when we were fourteen years old and through our teenage and young-married years. Somehow, life had tossed us about in different directions. But we never forgot one another.

Now we were getting together again. She was still married to the man she had fallen in love with, and I was now a widow. She came east to attend a wedding, and while she was here, we planned a visit. So many years had intervened. So much of life had already been lived. I wondered, *How could we catch up with all of it? Would there be enough time? Was the distance too long between the young girls who giggled all afternoon while listening to the phonograph, and the mothers and grandmothers we now were?*

Looking back, the problems we shared then, so urgent at the time, appeared less so now. Hours spent wondering if our bodies would ever change so that young men would be attracted to their curves. And when they did, other problems arrived. As we sat and painted fingernails together, daydreamed together, decided on the Saturday night date together, shopped for clothes together, we knew instinctively we could deal with all the changes, the frustrations and the uncertainties, together. I traveled nearly an hour to spend Sunday mornings in her kitchen having breakfast with her parents. They never knew why we were laughing or what we talked about at the table. She came to the shore to be with me, to sit on the sand, baking for hours, but with the silent understanding we didn't dare go in the water and get wet. That would have been disastrous to the image we had spent hours creating. To the world, we were popular and fun. To each other, we were real. Vulnerable and unsure.

We had seen each other last in the midst of life, children about our knees, energy in our eyes. I was thinking just before she arrived, *Would she not recognize me now?* I glanced into the mirror and surveyed the white hair, the lined face. *Would she be doing the same?*

When she stepped from the car, we spent many long moments just looking at one another. I knew then it didn't matter what we looked like. For neither of us would see it, anyway. "You look the same," I said, and I meant it. She said something similar to me. For in our laugh, our broad smiles, our loving eyes and warm hugs, nothing had changed.

Perhaps because love is ageless. And that's what had remained between us, the strong bond of friendship and the love that accompanied it. We both felt its power as we stood there, for those few moments in silence, just drinking in each other's presence.

She had kept our friendship alive through photographs, which she shared. One was of me in a bathing suit. On the back I had written that someday we would sit together, perhaps fifty years later, and my love for her would be the same. And it was over fifty years later that we were doing so. But my feelings were even deeper now. Sitting at my kitchen table, sharing tea and cake, talking about our children and grandchildren, our accomplishments in life, I realized we had more to give to one another than ever. More than ever, I appreciated the friendship that had survived so many years.

We laughed over the heartbreaking moment, at least for me, when she told me, on a street corner, after we had attended our college night classes, that she and the wonderful young man she loved were going to get married. "Married?" I asked, shocked. "You don't want to get married. Not yet." She was about twenty. And so was I. We were going to go to college at night. We had dreams to chase, together. Now she would seek them with someone else. And leave me to chase them alone.

Fifty years later, as the back of the photograph predicted, we were sitting around a table. It also predicted we wouldn't look the same.

To each other, we did.

Harriet May Savitz

More Chicken Soup?

Many of the stories and poems you have read in this book were submitted by readers like you who had read earlier *Chicken Soup for the Soul* books. We publish at least five or six *Chicken Soup for the Soul* books every year. We invite you to contribute a story to one of these future volumes.

Stories may be up to twelve hundred words and must uplift or inspire. You may submit an original piece, something you have read or your favorite quotation on your refrigerator door.

To obtain a copy of our submission guidelines and a listing of upcoming *Chicken Soup* books, please write, fax or check our Web site.

Please send your submissions to:

Chicken Soup for the Soul
P.O. Box 30880, Santa Barbara, CA 93130
fax: 805-563-2945
Web site: *www.chickensoupforthesoul.com*

We will be sure that both you and the author are credited for your submission.

For information about speaking engagements, other books, audiotapes, workshops and training programs, please contact any of our authors directly.

Who Is Jack Canfield?

Jack Canfield is one of America's leading experts in the development of human potential and personal effectiveness. He is both a dynamic, entertaining speaker and a highly sought-after trainer. Jack has a wonderful ability to inform and inspire audiences toward increased levels of self-esteem and peak performance.

He is the author and narrator of several bestselling audio- and videocassette programs, including *Self-Esteem and Peak Performance, How to Build High Self-Esteem, Self-Esteem in the Classroom* and *Chicken Soup for the Soul—Live.* He is regularly seen on television shows such as *Good Morning America, 20/20* and *NBC Nightly News.* Jack has co-authored numerous books, including the *Chicken Soup for the Soul* series, *Dare to Win* and *The Aladdin Factor* (all with Mark Victor Hansen), *100 Ways to Build Self-Concept in the Classroom* (with Harold C. Wells), *Heart at Work* (with Jacqueline Miller) and *The Power of Focus* (with Les Hewitt and Mark Victor Hansen).

Jack is a regularly featured speaker for professional associations, school districts, government agencies, churches, hospitals, sales organizations and corporations. His clients have included the American Dental Association, the American Management Association, AT&T, Campbell's Soup, Clairol, Domino's Pizza, GE, ITT, Hartford Insurance, Johnson & Johnson, the Million Dollar Roundtable, NCR, New England Telephone, Re/Max, Scott Paper, TRW and Virgin Records. Jack has taught on the faculty of Income Builders International, a school for entrepreneurs.

Jack conducts an annual seven-day Living Your Highest Vision training for entrepreneurs, educators, counselors, sales professionals, corporate trainers, professional speakers, ministers and others interested in creating and living their ideal lives.

For further information about Jack's books, tapes and training programs, or to schedule him for a presentation, please contact:

Self-Esteem Seminars
P.O. Box 30880
Santa Barbara, CA 93130
phone: 805-563-2935 • fax: 805-563-2945
Web site: *www.jackcanfield.com*

Who Is Mark Victor Hansen?

In the area of human potential, no one is more respected than Mark Victor Hansen. For more than thirty years, Mark has focused solely on helping people from all walks of life reshape their personal vision of what's possible. His powerful messages of possibility, opportunity and action have created powerful change in thousands of organizations and millions of individuals worldwide.

He is a sought-after keynote speaker, bestselling author and marketing maven. Mark's credentials include a lifetime of entrepreneurial success and an extensive academic background. He is a prolific writer, with many bestselling books such as *The One Minute Millionaire, The Power of Focus, The Aladdin Factor* and *Dare to Win,* in addition to the *Chicken Soup for the Soul* series. Mark has made a profound influence through his library of audios, videos and articles in the areas of big thinking, sales achievement, wealth building, publishing success, and personal and professional development.

Mark is the founder of the MEGA Seminar Series. MEGA Book Marketing University and Building Your MEGA Speaking Empire are annual conferences where Mark coaches and teaches new and aspiring authors, speakers and experts on building lucrative publishing and speaking careers. Other MEGA events include MEGA Marketing Magic and My MEGA Life.

He has appeared on television (*Oprah,* CNN and *The Today Show*), in print (*Time, U.S. News & World Report, USA Today, New York Times* and *Entrepreneur*) and on countless radio interviews, assuring our planet's people that "You can easily create the life you deserve."

As a philanthropist and humanitarian, Mark works tirelessly for organizations such as Habitat for Humanity, American Red Cross, March of Dimes, Childhelp USA and many others. He is the recipient of numerous awards that honor his entrepreneurial spirit, philanthropic heart and business acumen. He is a lifetime member of the Horatio Alger Association of Distinguished Americans, an organization that honored Mark with the prestigious Horatio Alger Award for his extraordinary life achievements.

Mark Victor Hansen is an enthusiastic crusader of what's possible and is driven to make the world a better place.

Mark Victor Hansen & Associates, Inc.
P.O. Box 7665
Newport Beach, CA 92658
phone: 949-764-2640
fax: 949-722-6912
Visit Mark online at: *www.markvictorhansen.com*

Who Are Chrissy and Mark Donnelly?

Chrissy and Mark Donnelly are a dynamic married couple working closely together as coauthors, marketers and speakers. They began their marriage with a decision to spend as much time together as possible—both in work and in spare time. During their honeymoon in 1995, they planned dozens of ways to leave their separate jobs and begin to work together on meaningful projects. Compiling a book of stories about love and romance was just one of the ideas.

Chrissy and Mark are the coauthors of the #1 *New York Times* best-sellers *Chicken Soup for the Couple's Soul, Chicken Soup for the Golfer's Soul, Chicken Soup for the Sports Fan's Soul, Chicken Soup for the Father's Soul, Chicken Soup for the Baseball Fan's Soul, Chicken Soup for the Golfer's Soul: The 2nd Round* and *Chicken Soup for the Romantic Soul.* They are also at work on several other upcoming books, among them *Chicken Soup for the Friend's Soul* and *Chicken Soup for the Married Soul.*

As cofounders of the Donnelly Marketing Group, they develop and implement innovative marketing and promotional strategies that help elevate and expand the *Chicken Soup for the Soul* message to millions of people around the world.

Chrissy, COO of the Donnelly Marketing Group, grew up in Portland, Oregon, and graduated from Portland State University. As a CPA, she embarked on a six-year career with Price Waterhouse.

Mark also grew up in Portland, Oregon, and unbeknownst to him, attended the same high school as Chrissy. He went on to graduate from the University of Arizona, where he was president of his fraternity, Alpha Tau Omega. He served as vice president of marketing for his family's business, Contact Lumber, and after eleven years resigned from day-to-day responsibilities to focus on his current endeavors.

Mark and Chrissy enjoy many hobbies together including golf, hiking, skiing, traveling, hip-hop aerobics and spending time with friends. Mark and Chrissy live in Paradise Valley, Arizona, and can be reached at:

Donnelly Marketing Group, LLC

3104 E. Camelback Road, Suite 531, Phoenix, AZ 85016

phone: 602-508-8956

fax: 602-508-8912

e-mail: *chickensoup@cox.net*

Who Is Stefanie Adrian?

Stefanie Adrian, an Indianapolis native who currently resides in San Diego, is one of the original panel members who read and rated stories for the first *Chicken Soup* book more than ten years ago.

Now, as coauthor of *Girlfriend's Soul*, she is delighted to celebrate the realization of a dream that was nearly seven years in the making. "The friendships that I have acquired in my life mean so much to me that I wanted to capture that meaning in a book," she explains. In working on this book, Stefanie not only learned perseverance and patience, but also met many new friends along the way.

"I also learned that every single person has a bond with at least one friend, and everyone has a special memory or story in which a friend's help made all the difference. You can't pick your family, but you can pick your friends," she says.

Stefanie is a freelance writer/editor who enjoys poetry and painting. She is also self-employed as a personal assistant, helping business clients with accounting and major-event planning. In addition, she helps individual clients with planning weddings and other major social events.

In her opinion, her most important job is being mom to her two sons: Keenan, eight, and Noah, seven. With that job comes all the fun of carpooling, the kids' sports and school activities. "I love that I am able to take them to and pick them up from school every day," she says. "That means a lot to me."

Stefanie is most thankful for her kids, her health, and the strength and courage with which God has blessed her. Such strength has allowed her to turn trials into opportunities. An example of her ability to do so is this book, born out of adversities faced during childhood. "Without friends, I wouldn't have survived," she says. "With them, all things are possible!"

Contributors

Several of the stories in this book were taken from previously published sources, such as books, magazines and newspapers. These sources are acknowledged in the permissions section. If you would like to contact any of the contributors for information about their writing or would like to invite them to speak in your community, look for their contact information included in their biographies.

The remainder of the stories were submitted by readers of our previous *Chicken Soup for the Soul* books who responded to our requests for stories. We have also included information about them.

Dee Adams' Web site (*www.minniepauz.com*) has been noted by many major newspapers such as *USA Today*, the *Los Angeles Times* and the *Detroit News*. She has been interviewed on ABC, NBC and PBS, as well as the site being shown on CNN. Valerie Harper says, "One of my favorites. . . . Click on and laugh your socks off. . . . You'll learn something, too!"

Suzanne A. Baginskie has worked as an office manager/paralegal in the same law firm for twenty-three years. She has several short stories and nonfiction articles published, and is currently working on a romantic suspense novel. Suzanne's hobbies include traveling, reading, daily walks and relaxing with a good movie. She and her husband, Al, reside on the west coast of Florida.

Benita Baker, a freelance writer from Ottawa, Canada, writes about people, culture and social history for magazines and newspapers. She has an MBA and an Honours BA in Canadian History and is the mother of two teenage boys. Visit her Web site at *http://members.rogers.com/benita.baker*.

Lana Brookman lives in her small Wisconsin hometown. She teaches for the area technical college and works part time for a small publisher. In her spare time, she likes to travel and enjoys time with her family and friends.

Debra Ayers Brown, president of Southeastern Writer's Association, is published in *Chicken Soup for the Expectant Mother's Soul, Guideposts, Woman's World*, the Chocolate and From the Heart series, and *From Eulogy to Joy*. More importantly, she is Meredith Brown's mom/chauffeur and wife of Allen Brown, all of Hinesville, Georgia. E-mail her at *www.dabmlb@clds.net*.

Stephanie Brush is the author of *Men: An Owner's Manual* (Simon & Schuster, 1984). She lives in Coeur d'Alene, Idaho, and currently works as a singer, actress and personal trainer.

Isabel Bearman Bucher and husband, Bob, both now retired, continue to rove the world doing home exchanging. Isabel writes stories of the heart, travel and just about anything that reaches out and grabs her. She's kept busy with her two grown daughters who frequently end up in text. She's beginning a new road—a fiction book that will take place in Taos, New Mexico, titled *Tafoya's Laundromat.*

Carol Bryant is a freelance writer whose topics include the concerns of the elderly and the people who care for them. She lives in Delaware with an extensive Tupperware collection. You can reach her at *carol33@gateway.net.*

Molly Noble Bull is married, the mother of three sons and a published author. She lives in the Texas Hill Country. Her historical novel, *The Winter Pearl,* will be published by Steeple Hill in November 2004. Visit her Web site at *www.mollybull.theaardvark.com.*

Marcia Byalick is a young-adult novelist and columnist for a Long Island magazine called *Distinction.* She loves working both as the content editor of *www.beinggirl.com,* a Web site for teenage girls, and a teacher of memoir writing for adults who want to get the story of their lives down on paper.

Melody Carlson is the award-winning author of more than a hundred books including *Finding Alice, Armando's Treasure, Angels in the Snow* and *Diary of a Teenage Girl.*

Teresa Cleary is a full-time mom and a part-time writer from Cincinnati, Ohio, where she lives with her husband, Tim, and their three children, Micah, Steven and Emily. She is the author of *Front Porch Reflections,* a woman's devotional book.

Phyllis Cochran, an inspirational published freelance writer since 1991, lives in Winchendon, Massachusetts, with her husband, Phil. Phyllis enjoys traveling with Phil and spending time with their grown children and grandchildren. She looks forward to seeing her book, *Shades of Light: A Mother & Daughter's Journey with God,* in print.

Helen Colella is a former teacher, mother of five and a freelance writer of stories and articles for adults and children as well as educational materials. She has been previously published in other *Chicken Soup for the Soul* books. Her new interest is in e-publishing and she offers her experience to those also interested in this area. Please reach her at *HCColella@aol.com.*

Alice Collins, mother of five and grandmother of twelve, resides in Oak Lawn with her husband, John, of forty-four years. From love's first kiss on a Schwinn bicycle to holding hands while saying grace around the family dinner table—family members now numbering twenty-four—family life and the gift of friendship have provided this writer and professional speaker with ever-growing material, laughter and love.

A retired English and journalism teacher, **Marjorie Conder** has always enjoyed reading and writing. Now she keeps busy with freelance writing and editing newsletters as well as enjoying her three grown children, eight grandchildren and eight plus great-grandchildren. She and her husband summer in northern Arizona and winter in Phoenix.

P. Audrey Conway retired after thirty-plus years of teaching and counseling high school students in central Pennsylvania. She enjoys her family activities, especially those of her two grandchildren, and is an avid reader and sports fan. You may contact her by e-mail at *conwayaw@aol.com*.

Shae Cooke, a Canadian inspirational writer, mother and former foster child, shares her heart and God's message of hope internationally. Contact her at PO Box 78006, Port Coquitlam, BC, Canada V3B 7H5 or e-mail *shaesy2000@yahoo.com* or see *www.bcfdf.com/thewriters/shaecooke/home.html*.

David Cooney's cartoon and illustrations appear in numerous *Chicken Soup for the Soul* books as well as magazines including *First for Women* and *Good Housekeeping*. David is a work-from-home dad, cartoonist, illustrator and photographer. David and his wife Marcia live in the small Pennsylvania town of Mifflinburg with their two children, Sarah and Andrew. David's Web site is *www.DavidCooney.com*. He can be reached at *david@davidcooney.com*.

Beth Dieselberg is a poet, writer, world traveler and lover of language. She received her bachelor of arts in Spanish and Portuguese from Indiana University. She is currently using her bilingual skills in the social service sector. Please e-mail her at *bdieselb@hotmail.com*.

Shari Dowdall is a wife and mother and works at a community college in Overland Park, Kansas. Shari's faith journey has been strengthened by her life experiences. Shari does volunteer work and enjoys helping others, taking walks, cooking classes, yoga and traveling. Please e-mail her at *shdowdal@jccc.net*.

Sue Dunigan has flourished as an inspirational speaker for over twenty years around the world. She loves living with her husband of over thirty years in the U.S. Virgin Islands. Her heart sings over her son, Nathaniel, who is founder and director of Aidchild in East Africa and her daughter, Hannah, who is working, studying and serving others in Phoenix, Arizona. E-mail her at *sue@aidchild.org*.

Sally Friedman, a graduate of the University of Pennsylvania, began writing essays three decades ago. She has contributed to the *New York Times, Family Circle, Bride's, Home* and other national publications. She lives in New Jersey. E-mail her at *pinegander@aol.com*.

Nancy B. Gibbs is an author, religion columnist and writer. She is a minister's wife, a mother and a grandmother. She has been published in several *Chicken Soup* books. Nancy has contributed to numerous anthologies, magazines and devotional guides. Contact her at *Daiseydood@aol.com* and *www.nancybgibbs.com.*

Jill Goldstein writes about her personal experiences in the hopes of providing inspiration and insight. She likes to spend time with friends and family. Jill lives in Princeton, New Jersey, with her two children Hanna and Harris.

Janna L. Graber is a freelance journalist who has written for publications like *Reader's Digest,* the *Chicago Tribune, Redbook* and *Family Circle.* She is currently a senior editor at *Go World Travel* magazine (*www.goworldtravel.com*), an international publication covering the world's most fascinating people and places.

Bill Holton is a freelance writer living in Florida.

Virelle Kidder is a full-time conference speaker, author of four books and former radio talk show host. Her newest book, *Donkeys Still Talk* (Navpress, 2004), is about hearing God's voice when you're not even listening. Virelle and her husband, Steve, have four grown children and live in Albany, New York. Visit her at *www.virellekidder.com* or *www.donkeysstilltalk.com.*

Karen R. Kilby resides in Kingwood, Texas, with her husband, David. As a certified personality trainer with CLASServices, Inc., Karen enjoys helping people understand themselves and others through her seminar presentations. Karen is also a speaker for Christian women's clubs with Stonecroft Ministries. Please reach her at *krkilby@kingwoodcable.net.*

Marlene L. King, M.A. is a writer, artist and mental health professional whose inspirational stories have appeared in the bestselling *Chocolate for a Woman's Soul* series, *Intuition Magazine* and *StressFree Living.* She writes an interactive column, "Dream Times," for *Dream Network Journal* and is currently marketing her second screenplay. E-mail her at *marlene@chatlink.com.*

Marylane Wade Koch is a freelance author and editor with *www. athomewithwords.com.* She has several books and numerous articles to her credit, mostly in the health care field. Professional memberships include the National League of American Penwomen Inc. and American Christian Writers. She chairs her local Christian writers' group in Byhalia, Mississippi.

Marian Lewis received her B.S. degree in nursing from the University of Oregon in 1942. She spent fifty years in nursing, with time out when her children were young. Her special pleasures are gardening, grand-parenting and writing. She writes stories, short essays and is developing a book based on her nursing experiences. Her e-mail is *marian2@surewest.net.*

Barbara LoMonaco received her Bachelor of Science degree from the University of Southern California and taught elementary school. After her sons were born, she "retired" from teaching and became a full-time stay-at-home mom. Barbara now works for Chicken Soup for the Soul as the assistant manager of acquisitions.

Patricia Lorenz is a full-time freelance writer and speaker who works out of her home in Oak Creek, Wisconsin. She's one of the top contributors to the *Chicken Soup* books with stories in eighteen of them. She's the author of five of her own books, including her three newest: *Great American Outhouse Stories: The Hole Truth and Nothing Butt; Life's Too Short to Fold Your Underwear* and *Grab the Extinguisher, My Birthday Cake's on Fire.* To contact Patricia for a speaking opportunity, e-mail *patricialorenz@juno.com.*

Anne Merle is a freelance writer living in Evanston, Illinois. Her Health and Family features appear in Chicago area Pioneer Press newspapers; travel articles at *www.TravelingToday.com;* director's column and theatrical commentary in trade papers *ITVA News* and *Performink.* Mother of two, she's also a professional actress. Contact her at *casamerle@aol.com.*

Roberta Messner, R.N., Ph.D., is a writer with over one thousand stories to her credit. Her work has appeared in a number of previous *Chicken Soup* editions.

Jane Milburn, a mother of three, lives with her husband on a small farm in central British Columbia. She loves farm life, gardening and spending time with her family and friends. She does day care and supports a person with mental handicaps in her home.

Janet Lynn Mitchell is a wife, mother, author and inspirational speaker. She is the coauthor of *A Special Kind of Love: For Those Who Love Children with Special Needs,* published by Broadman and Holman and Focus on the Family, 2004. Janet can be reached at *Janetlm@prodigy.net.* or via fax (714) 633-6309.

Jenna Marie Mitchell is a freshman in college. She loves spending time with her family and friends. Music is her passion. Her life's goal is to serve God, her creator.

Since retiring as a reading specialist from the Pittsburgh schools, **Polly Moran** is a published writer. She's sold over fifty stories and articles. Currently, Polly has an editor waiting to read her romance novel. She enjoys traveling, theater, both on and off stage, and spending time with her six grandchildren.

Wendi R. Morris lives with her husband, Herb, in Boca Raton, Florida. She divides her time between designing handcrafted art cards and picture frames and enjoying precious time with her three grandchildren. She is currently authoring various children's books and novels. Please e-mail her at *wendiwrap@bellsouth.net.*

Marguerite Murer is an educator, a professional speaker and an aspiring author. Drawing on her unique experiences from teaching high school, working for the Texas Rangers Baseball Club and serving in the White House, she finds inspiration in all Americans. You may reach Marguerite at *megmurer@aol.com.*

Jennifer Nicholson is a Canadian wife and mother of two with a B.S. degree in biochemistry from the University of Ottawa. Jenn enjoys spending time with her family and friends, scrapbooking, travel and is a perpetual student of life. An up-and-coming writer, she is especially interested in promoting children's literacy.

Mary Treacy O'Keefe, M.A., is cofounder and spiritual director at Well Within, a Minnesota wellness resource center that supports people in health crises. Mary loves to speak about soul friendships, like the one between Agnes Krenik and CeCe Cashin. Watch for her new book, *Thin Places.* Contact Mary at *mtokeefe@comcast.net.*

Vivia M. Peterson is a registered nurse who has been in the nursing profession for twenty-nine years. Currently, she is a quality improvement and compliance manager in Northern California. Vivia enjoys antiquing, swimming, traveling, volunteering in her church, and spending time with her husband, family and friends. Her grandchildren are the joy of her life.

Carol McAdoo Rehme, one of *Chicken Soup's* most prolific contributors, believes that girlfriends pick you up, prop you up and lift you up. Carol directs a nonprofit, Vintage Voices, Inc., which brings interactive programming to the vulnerable elderly. Contact her at *carol@rehme.com;* or see *www.rehme.com.*

Carol J. Rhodes's work, poetry, short stories, essays and nonfiction have been widely published since she began writing in 1992. She teaches business communication workshops for the University of Houston (her alma mater) and a creative writing class for The Women's Institute. Her first book, *Where Have They Gone?*, is scheduled for publication in 2004.

A writer and educator, **Deborah Ritz** received her bachelor of arts from Dickinson College and master of teaching from the University of Richmond. She is employed at the Virginia Museum of Fine Arts and facilitates creative writing and art workshops for children and adults. Deborah can be reached at *dr@moonlitwaters.com.*

Harriet May Savitz has had twenty-two books published and an ABC Afterschool Special produced by Henry Winkler. Her recent book of essays, *Dear Daughter and Sons,* is a tribute to the military. Other works can be seen on her Web site at *www.harrietmaysavitz.com.* She can be reached by e-mail at *hmaysavitz@aol.com.*

Jodi L. Severson earned a bachelor's degree from the University of Pittsburgh.

She resides in Wisconsin with her husband and three children. Her stories have appeared in other *Chicken Soup* books including *Sister's Soul, Working Woman's Soul* and *Chicken Soup Celebrates Sisters.* Several biographies she has written have been published in *US Legacies* magazine, and she is currently seeking a publisher for a children's book she's written. Reach her at *jodis@charter.net.*

Kathy Shaskan is an artist and writer living in New Jersey.

Beth Sherrow grew up in Lexington, Kentucky, and lived in Versailles, Kentucky, for twenty years. Beth is married and has three sons ages twenty-three, eighteen and twelve. Beth is the office manager for T'Bred horse farm in Ocala, Florida.

Bohne Goldfarb Silber was born and raised in Memphis, Tennessee, and lives in Maryland with her husband and four children. She holds a Ph.D. in psychology and owns a social science research company. Please e-mail her at *bgsilber@hotmail.com.*

Wendy Simmerman has a B.A. and M.A. in theater from Brigham Young University. Her theatrical work has been performed in various venues worldwide. She enjoys teaching and freelance writing, although her primary passion is being a mom to her beautiful children. If her story has touched you, please e-mail her at *wjsimms@aol.com.*

Lizanne Southgate is a writer, award-winning photographer and mother. Like Whitman, she believes that "much unseen is also here." E-mail her at *lizannes@exchangenet.net.*

Jennifer Stevens works full time in marketing and sales for a multicultural children's book publisher called Lee & Low Books and part time as a reporter for a weekly newspaper called the *Times Newsweekly.* She lives in Queens, New York. She can be reached by e-mail at *jlyn2677@aol.com.*

Monika Szamko received a business degree from Northeastern University, and an M.B.A. from MIT. She lives in San Francisco and works for an international nonprofit focused on alleviating poverty in Africa. Monika enjoys traveling, skiing and painting. She is working on two adventure novels. Please e-mail her at: *monika_szamko@hotmail.com.*

Andrew Toos has provided editorially on-target cartoons for print and electronic media since 1984. He has established a national and international reputation through his off-beat lifestyle cartoons for clients such as: *Reader's Digest, Saturday Evening Post, Gallery, Stern, Accountancy, Baseball Digest, CEO, The Washington Post, Barron's,* Bayer Corp, *Good Housekeeping, Cosmopolitan* and many other titles and media outlets. In addition to his lifestyle cartoons, he also creates work on employment, medical/healthcare, computer, business, travel, hobby, mature adult, teen, children's and entertainment themes. He provides the widest range of stock cartoons available through his Web site at: *www.cartoonresource.com*.

A writer and speaker, **PeggySue Wells** coauthored books including *What to Do When You Don't Know What to Say* and *What to Do When You Don't Want to Go to Church*. Author of the Gaither Pond Unit Studies, PeggySue homeschools and travels with her seven musical children, The WELLSpring Fiddlers.

Janet Hall Wigler started writing for a newspaper owned and operated by her mother, Angela Hall, in Bella Coola, British Columbia. She has since gone on to write plays, short stories and has just completed her second novel. Janet lives in California with her husband, Greg.

Phyllis W. Zeno is the founding editor of *AAA Going Places* and just retired after twenty-nine years as creative director of AAA Auto Club South. She and her daughter, Linda W. Aber, are the coauthors of *Look, Find & Learn: US History* and *Look, Find & Learn: World History*. She was a contributor to *Chicken Soup for the Mother & Daughter Soul,* and is an active travel and freelance writer. You may contact her at *Phylliszeno@aol.com.*

Permissions *(continued from page iv)*

The Swing. Reprinted by permission of Teresa J. Cleary ©1989. Teresa J. Cleary.

Power of Love and *As Close as Sisters.* Reprinted by permission of Bill Holton. ©2002 Bill Holton.

Flowers from Our Garden. From *EARTH ANGELS* by Jerry Biederman and Lorin Biederman, ©1997 by Jerry Biederman and Lorin Biederman. Used by permission of Broadway Books, a division of Random House, Inc.

The Wonders of Tupperware. Reprinted by permission of Carol Bryant. ©2000 Carol Bryant.

The Tablecloth. Reprinted by permission on Bohne Goldfarb Silber. ©1999 Bohne Goldfarb Silber.

I've Fallen and I Can't Get Up and *That's What Friends Are For.* Reprinted by permission of Phyllis W. Zeno. ©1996 Phyllis W. Zeno.

May Baskets. Reprinted by permission of Sue Dunigan. ©1990 Sue Dunigan.

Change of Heart. Reprinted by permission of Jane Milburn. ©1998 Jane Milburn.

Operation: Heart Attack. Reprinted by permission of Wendy Simmerman. ©1998 Wendy Simmerman.

Birthday Presents. Reprinted by permission of Marguerite Murer. ©2003 Marguerite Murer.

In Praise of Best Girlfriends. Reprinted by permission of Stephanie Brush. ©1991 Stephanie Brush.

To Pee or Not to Pee. Reprinted by permission of Marcia Byalick. ©2003 Marcia Byalick.

Half the Fun Is Getting There. Reprinted by permision of Janet Mitchell ©2002 Janet Mitchell.

Christine's Comfort Shower. Reprinted by permission of Deborah Miller Ritz. ©2003 Deborah Miller Ritz.

A Good Connection. Reprinted by permission of Anne Merle. ©2002 Anne Merle.

Opening Doors. Reprinted by permission of Janna Graber. ©2004 Janna Graber.

Got Tea? Reprinted by permission of PeggySue Wells. ©2003 PeggySue Wells.

Details. Reprinted by permission of Lizanne Southgate. ©2001 Lizanne Southgate.

Famous Last Words. Reprinted by permission of Barbara LoMonaco. ©2003 Barbara LoMonaco.

Knowing When. Reprinted by permission of Helen Colella. ©2003 Helen Colella.

Guaranteed to make you smile!

Take time for you

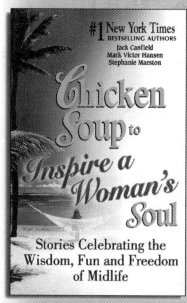

A dose of inspiration

#1 New York Times **BESTSELLING AUTHORS**
Jack Canfield
Mark Victor Hansen
LeAnn Thieman, L.P.N.
*with a Foreword
by Rosalynn Carter*

Chicken Soup for the Caregiver's Soul

Stories to Inspire Caregivers
in the Home, the Community
and the World

Code 1592 • Paperback • $12.95

#1 New York Times **BESTSELLING AUTHORS**
Jack Canfield
Mark Victor Hansen
Arline McGraw Oberst
John T. Boal
Tom & Laura Lagana

Chicken Soup for the Volunteer's Soul

With Stories About:
American Red Cross
Big Brothers Big Sisters
Habitat for Humanity
Peace Corps
Points of Light
Rotary
And Many More

Stories to Celebrate
the Spirit of Courage,
Caring and Community

Code 0146 • Paperback • $12.95

NEW from the creators of
Chicken Soup for the Soul

From the Creators of
Chicken Soup for the Soul

Life Lessons for Women

7 Essential Ingredients for a Balanced Life

Stephanie Marston, M.F.T.

Jack Canfield and Mark Victor Hansen

Code 1444 • Paperback • $12.95

An exciting new series combining practical advice with powerful stories, Life Lessons overflows with inspiration and direction for creating a significant life.